THE MYSTERIES
OF CHARTRES
CATHEDRAL

Also translated by Ronald Fraser
HER BAK, EGYPTIAN INITIATE
by Isha Schwaller de Lubicz

THE MYSTERIES OF CHARTRES CATHEDRAL

by

Louis Charpentier

English translation by Ronald Fraser
in collaboration with Janette Jackson

RESEARCH INTO LOST KNOWLEDGE
ORGANISATION

RILKO BOOKS
'Windings'
New England Lane
Playden, Nr. Rye
E. Sussex TN31 7NT
Tel & Fax: 01797 226723

Originally published by Robert Laffont,
6 place Saint-Sulpice, Paris-VI, France

First English Edition August 1972
Second Impression July 1975
Third Impression March 1980
Fourth Impression December 1983
Fifth Impression December 1988
Sixth Impression December 1993
Seventh Impression April 1997
Eight Impression May 1999
Ninth Impression May 2002

ISBN 0 902103 16 4

Printed and bound in Great Britain

Printed by Athenæum Press Ltd, Gateshead, Tyne & Wear

TABLE OF CONTENTS

Publisher's Foreword

Our knowledge of the past, ancient and mediaeval, is growing. Our views on a number of archaeological and historical problems are expanding. Now M. Charpentier opens a fresh vista of possibilities. He says in effect that Chartres and other cathedrals, like the great monuments of Egypt and Greece, were the manifestation of a secret communicated to mankind by occult or mystical means. This, he claims, required the services of a man equipped to receive a Dedication in occult language; a man competent to translate the message into numbers and a master-craftsman who knew what he was about and could express such numbers or relationships in curves, verticals and volumes. Moreover, the secret of true gothic was communicated to man with a view to a fuller realisation of his own quality.

In answer to various requests, it was decided that efforts be made to get the book published in English and Sir Ronald Fraser made the necessary translation. It was due to the generosity of an anonymous American friend that the English-speaking rights were purchased for R.I.L.K.O., and for this grace we are very grateful.

Janette Jackson

SIR RONALD FRASER KBE, CMG

AN APPRECIATION

The French original of this book was given to Mrs Janette Jackson by the late J.G. Bennett. She immediately realized its impact as an 'opener of windows', and it must be stated that but for her initiative and persistence the whole scheme would never have got off the ground. She asked the late Sir Ronald Fraser to do a translation, and he generously agreed to this for it accorded with his own way of thought.

The work was completed some time before funds were available to publish an edition in English, and there began a race between time and Sir Ronald's increasing blindness and frailty. His family recall how he sat daily at his desk struggling to read galley proofs with one eye and a magnifying glass. Thanks to his gallant determination and the help of his friends the task was completed, and of all his literary achievements (and he had over thirty published books to his name) this work on Chartres Cathedral became the one with which he was happiest to be associated.

It is perhaps typical of the whole spirit of the enterprise that neither Janette Jackson nor Ronald Fraser accepted any remuneration for their services. For both of them the interest which the labour aroused was their reward.

Sir Ronald is also known for his scholarly translation of *Her Bak, Egyptian Initiate*, written by the late Isha Schwaller de Lubicz (Hodder and Stoughton), and it is worthy of remark that her husband, the late R.A. Schwaller de Lubicz, Egyptologist and mystic, uncovered the mysteries of Luxor in much the same way as did Louis Charpentier those of Chartres Cathedral.

Sir Ronald Fraser died on 12 September 1974, nearing his eighty-sixth birthday. He is owed a debt of gratitude and appreciation.

1 A Spot of Sunlight

There is in Chartres Cathedral, in the western aisle of the south transept, a rectangular flagstone, set aslant to the others, whose whiteness is noticeable in the prevailing grey of the paving. It is conspicuous for a shining, lightly gilded metal tenon.

Every year, on 21st June, when the sun is bright, as is usual at that time of year, a ray strikes this stone at midday precisely; a ray that comes through a contrived space in the stained-glass window named for Saint Apollinaire, first on the western side of the transept. All the guides point this out and it is accepted as a whim on the part of the paviour, glazier, or builder.

Chance having brought me to Chartres one 21st June, I formed the wish to see this curiosity, among other curiosities of the place.

In my reckoning, local midday would fall between a quarter and five minutes to 1 p.m. as shewn by our watches. It was exactly then that the ray illuminated the stone.

What is especially astonishing about a ray of sunshine that casts a spot of light on the ground in a shadowy place? One sees it every day. Still, I could not rid myself of a feeling that there was something strange. Someone, at some time in the past, had taken the trouble to leave an empty space, minute perhaps, in a stained-glass window. Someone else had taken the trouble to pick out a particular flagstone, different from the rest of those which constitute the floor of the cathedral, whiter, with a view to its being noticed. He had taken the trouble to prepare a place of the right size for it, slantwise, and set it there; to drill a hole for the tenon of lightly gilded metal, which marked neither the middle of the flagstone nor one of its axes. Here we have rather more than a stone-mason's whim. One does not make a hole in a stained-glass window to throw light on a flagstone on particular days in the year. Neither does a glazier change the position of a flagstone merely to point out the omission of a bit of glass from a window he has just set in place.

A concerted intention was at the bottom of this. Stone-mason and glazier obeyed an order. And this order was given with a view to a specific time: the only moment in the year when a ray of the sun can fall on the flagstone is the summer solstice, when the sun reaches the climax of its northern journey. It was given them by an astronomer.

And in relation to a particular spot. The flagstone lies in a prolongation of the south wall of the nave, in the middle of the aisle, yet not exactly at the centre; the inclination of the slab was certainly intended. The place was chosen by a geometer.

When this little game of 'the sun on the slab' is played in one of the most venerated cathedrals of the West, in one of the places of highest fame in France, the idea takes hold of you that there is a mystery. It took hold of me.

What was it that had escaped the Directors of Patronage, the 'right-thinking' of the catechism, theology, or of the Golden Legend? What was this warning? All of a sudden everything was full of mystery. The cathedral took a life of its own, a life that puzzled me without, for all that, being alien. Everything seemed at the same time strange and familiar. This vault, with which, in some sense, I did not feel out of proportion, was higher than a house of twelve stories. This cathedral, so quickly traversed, could have contained a stadium. It would have taken four men with arms outstretched to encircle these columns, so perfectly proportioned that they seemed normal. And nothing in any part of the cathedral seemed more than human, nothing seemed outside man's range. How strange!

Thus, though it all turned mysterious, I was far from feeling the discomfort that troubled me on the threshold of the temple at Edfu, where colossal pylons seem to repel you as if they would drive man from a world where he has no place. Here on the contrary the half-light was magical with bright rays. Everything contained its opposite in itself. Immensity welcomed you. Height, far from crushing you, seemed to induce growth. Although the sun stood in the south, it was the Rose in the north transept that glowed with a thousand fires. The tall figures of Saint Anne of the Black Face, holding both the Lily and the Virgin, of Solomon and David, of Melchisedek and Aaron, though immobile were alive with light; though hierarchs they were familiar as the figures in a child's picture-book. Childlike; yet at the same time skill in line and colour dispelled any impression of naivety.

What then was this magic I felt so near to under-standing; this spell whose secret was going to be disclosed to me, now, here, near the stone on which the sun had written, for an instant, its round shape?

There was a moment, a lightning-flash, when I thought I had understood Chartres, the mysteries of her stones and bright jewels; but it was Chartres that had me in its grasp.

Doors, however, are not opened without a key nor without a keyword. One had to look for them.

It is difficult to say just when research becomes a vice, as happens to those who do crossword puzzles; but the fact is that I had stuck my finger into the machinery and the rest followed; the study of works that specialise in architectural design, the erection of theses soon to be destroyed by comparisons of dates, enthusiasms turning to discouragement. I found myself deep, sometimes to the point of suffocation, in a research which sprang from time past into present space . . .

It would be tedious to describe the tortuous paths I followed; tedious as the hours spent with a table of logarithms which I thought I had left behind with my schooldays. Nevertheless, I now hand over the result of this enquiry, this quest, in the hope that it will interest some of my contemporaries.

For most people it is only the unaccustomed that is mysterious. Who would think of marvelling over what he sees every day? Those who lived on the banks of the Nile saw nothing mysterious in the hundreds of pyramids that bordered their river. They were told that they were tombs and it was enough for them.

For visitors, the cathedral at Chartres is but one gothic monument among others; less mysterious indeed than many because it has almost none of those medallions or images whose alchemical significance has been so learnedly shewn by the Adept Fulcanelli.

Yet what mysteries! The more difficult to clarify because there is a hiatus between the men of that time and ourselves, a gulf in which a form of civilisation has disappeared. What was a civilisation has gone up in a dust-cloud of particulars.

Notwithstanding deceptive spaces of time, the distance between the builders of cathedrals and the men of the Renaissance is greater than that between these last and ourselves. Most of the mysteries at Chartres are only mysteries for us, twentieth century men, who, as regards men of past ages have only prefabricated ideas, ideas prefabricated by scholars.

If we confine ourselves to gothic art, this alone puts a question to which no answer has ever been given. We know all about romanesque origins; we follow the path from monument to monument, period to period; but the gothic has always eluded attempts to fix its origin. The historic question remains posed. It appears suddenly, without preamble, towards 1130. In a few years it reaches its apogee, born whole and entire without experiment or miscarriage. And the extraordinary thing is that all at once it has at its disposal master-craftsmen, artisans, builders, enough of them to undertake the construction of eighty huge monuments in less than a hundred years.

Historians are astonishing people. One sometimes has the impression that they never ask themselves questions. Perhaps it is their training, which is romantic. Very few people are able to rid themselves of the idea that Art is a thing in itself. Or that Art, which should be the expression of a man's personality, is only this. It affords pleasure to those who manufacture objects of art, still more to those who traffic in them. This is why 'the gothic' is reduced to the rank of a mere fashion. Men wrought in the gothic style because this was the mode, just as at one time the mode was romanesque.

However, the men who built Chartres certainly never thought merely to enliven the horizontal country of La Beauce with a vertical shaft. They would never have undertaken to build a cathedral if they had not thought it 'useful' to do so and it would be astonishing if they had not viewed the enterprise as 'rational'. All that we do not understand, all that seems mysterious to us or that we see as an architect's or a sculptor's whim, had its *raison d'être*, a utilitarian one, even if we cannot guess what its utility was. It is not the result of chance, even artistic chance, that the church stands where it does; it is not by chance that its orientation is unusual for a catholic edifice. Its ogive, its breadth, length and height, do not proceed from the reflections of an aesthete. The relations of length, breadth and height were not planned to make the church look pretty; they result from a *necessity* which the builders could not escape, something 'outside' themselves. In the same way the ogive proceeds from a necessity which is moreover less architectural than physiological; and those famous windows, which no-one has ever been able to analyse or reproduce, and which possess such extraordinary qualities of light, were conceived under necessity. Everything is designed to act on a man, on mankind; everything, to the last detail: the labyrinth now littered with chairs, the flagstone on which the midday sun casts a spot of light at the summer solstice.

And there is another aspect of the question which people are apt to forget. It is that all these things, whole or part, were brought into being by men who *knew* what they were about. Mystery adds to mystery — we do not know who they were or whence their knowledge came. It was very great. Notre Dame de Chartres is seven hundred years old. The church has suffered, apart from the inescapable damage of time, at least one serious fire; yet there has never been any need to strengthen, shore up or restore, save in some matters of detail. And these amazing architects who conceived the church, the builders who built it — we simply do not know them. In fact we know so little that we may ask ourselves sometimes whether a mystery was not woven about them for some political or other reason; whether it was not willed from the start, to screen them from enquiry or, perhaps, from the Inquisition?

I will mention for what it is worth the explanation put out by the Directors of Patronage, that all this has no other source than Faith. Faith may remove mountains, and these men undoubtedly had it; but it calls for something more to poise the largest known gothic vault, and one of the highest. It calls for knowledge.

Well then, a fresh mystery. Where did they get it? The Middle Ages are always presented to us as a time of obscurantism — there is nothing but what is false in this assertion. It is the age of the crusade against the

Albigenses; the birth of the Dominican inquisition; it is the age of the stake. How are we to reconcile it all?

Cluny is explained by its scholarly monks – but not Chartres, Amiens, Sens, Reims, about which there is nothing monkish, for these are popular shrines, built for the people, by laymen; by men of this ignorant people, that is. We ask how they can have furnished carpenters, masons, stone-cutters, sculptors, scholars, in the numbers required for the building of these immense vessels of stone. One has to bear in mind that in northern France alone, at the time Chartres was being built, nearly twenty cathedrals of the same importance were under construction. And how many smaller churches? All done by hand, if I may venture to say it; by hand, human muscle activating the human hand as the only driving-power. And one must also remember that there cannot have been much more than fifteen million inhabitants in the whole of France.

And now another mystery. How was it all financed? In spite of their faith the workers cannot have worked without pay. And historians are in agreement that the people were needy, which is certainly true. Whence, then, the funds?

From donors? Their names are in the record. They gave – one an altar, one a retable, another a stained-glass window. Trifles in such a totality.

There were offerings, collections, no doubt; sometimes taxes were imposed on the markets; for Chartres, there were the pilgrims. But pilgrims did not carry gold in their scrips. And sales in a small borough cannot have been considerable.

Well then, one must try to think logically, at least as regards matters that are amenable to human logic. Thus, this flowering of cathedrals must have been *willed*.

It must have been willed by an organisation with the requisite knowledge; which had competent builders at its disposal and the means to finance them. Finally, and this is obvious, it must have been of a religious order.

But the secular clergy, the bishops, canons and priests, had neither the knowledge nor, apart from the great metropolitan sees, the means. Only the monastic Orders, above all the Benedictines and Cistercians, had at that time the knowledge, the means and the builders; but they reserved it all for their Abbeys. It was neither Cluny nor Citeaux that made Chartres.

We fall from one mystery into another.

And again one more: why this huge, magnificent church in the mere borough that was Chartres? Why this church for the building of which, we cannot doubt it, the best among the best master-craftsmen, masons, stone-cutters, sculptors and carpenters were mobilised? Was Chartres privileged?

2 The Mystery of the Mound*

The cathedral of Chartres stands on an eminence whose history remains in many respects mysterious. In Christian times it was one of the most sought-after places of pilgrimage in France; but before that the Gauls went there in crowds and still earlier the whole Celtic world, even from beyond the Rhine.

Pilgrims of the Christian era, those of the Great Pilgrimage, who came from the East, entered the town by the Porte Guillaume not far from which they were received at the 'hospital' of the Benedictine monastery whose Abbey is now the church of Saint Peter. Here they were lodged, refreshed, cherished; then, having prayed in the Abbey, heard matins and mass, they went up singing psalms to do homage to Our Lady of Under-the-Earth, the Black Virgin, in whose honour they had taken the pilgrim's staff and cape.

Next, they went in procession, by a passage on the north side which leads to the crypt, to visit a grotto, underneath the church, where the sacred statue was to be seen. Having punctiliously made their devotions and having been asperged with water from a well which opens in the crypt, of which they likewise drank, they walked in procession, still underground, round the vault of Saint Lubin and emerged by the southern passage.

* The French word is 'tertre' (Celtic 'tert') for which we have no equivalent in English unless we use tump, hillock, knoll, mound or tor.

In the evening they listened to the story of the Black
Virgin. The statue, carved in the hollowed-out trunk of a
pear tree and very ancient, represented the Holy Virgin,
seated with the Infant God on her knees. Age had
blackened it, for it was made, not by Christians but before
the birth of the Saviour by Druids, pagan priests to whom
a prophetic angel announced that a Virgin would give birth
to a God; and it was thus that they portrayed her, as she
was to be, with great devotion and on the pedestal they
wrote, in fine Roman lettering, the words 'Virgini
pariturae', meaning, 'The Virgin who will give birth to a
Child'.

When the first Christians came to Chartres they found
this statue and were amazed. They conceived a deep
reverence for this prophetic Virgin and they continued to
call the cave where they found her 'the Druid grotto', and
without knowing why, they called the well on one side of it
'The Well of the Strong', a name it had kept through the
ages.

What the pilgrims perhaps did not know was that they
had merely taken a road that generations on generations
had taken before them; for the pilgrimage to Chartres was
made long before the Christians, probably long before the
Celts. Generations and generations before them came to
meditate in the grotto where a Virgin Mother reigned, a
Black Virgin who was named Isis perhaps, or Demeter, or
Bélisama.

Thanks to Henri Dontenville (author of 'French Mythology'), we know what route the Great Pilgrimage took,
coming from the East via Raon-l'Etape and the place that
became Sainte-Odile; a route which was also that of the
pilgrimage to Mont-Tombe, now Mont-Saint-Michel. They
came a long way to reach this spot, this mound, where
Earth dispensed gifts. For the prime mystery of Chartres is
its situation, which conceals one of nature's most extraordinary secrets, one that affects the very life of men.

Let us spare a thought for those who century after century, millennium after millennium, took the pilgrim's staff, whether they were pagan or Christian, faced dangers now only met with in stories for children, and set out by roads which were hardly tracks, across rivers that were hardly fordable, through forests where the wolf hunted in packs, through marshes of shifting mud in which poisonous water-snakes lurked; men who were subjected to rain, wind, storms, sharp hail, sunstruck or frozen, at night their only shelter a flap of their tunic pulled over the head; all this having left home and family not knowing if they would see them again, in order to reach at least once in their lives a place where a divinity dwelt.

What exactly were they looking for? Did they mean to do penance? Penance is specifically Christian and the pilgrimage dates from before Christianity. They must then have known that they would meet in the place of pilgrimage with some quality, some beneficent influence.

In those times, no more than today, still less perhaps, a man did not go on pilgrimage without hope of advantage. One goes in search of something one cannot have by staying at home. One seeks the Gift of Earth; something Earth gives like a Mother.

One goes on pilgrimage as to a cure. The sick resort to places where the water, or even the mud, issuing from the ground, has healing power. A pilgrimage being essentially a religious exercise, it is a religious advantage that is sought. It is Spirit that one wishes to find.

There are, said Barrès, places where one breathes in spirit, places where a man can steep himself in it, or, if you prefer, where he quickens the sense of the divine in himself. This is the greatest gift of Earth and Heaven to man.

Among the ancients, man was truly man only when his spiritual faculties were awakened. This could come about by inward grace, by asceticism, by rhythmic or somatic spell; but a place apart has always been reserved for the awakening acquired by terrestrial action in places of pilgrimage; ancient and modern being generally, normally, the same. More sensitive than we to the action and properties of natural forces, the ancients knew such places much better than we do and if we want to find them again we are reduced to searching among the clues they left, megaliths, dolmens or temples. Chartres is certainly such a place.

To men of the twentieth century such a phrase as 'the spirit that breathes or inspires' may sound childish; but this is only because metaphors and images have changed. One can designate 'spirit' in learned enough terms, but it would be a pity not to recall the old Gaulish name for it, *Wouivre*.

The *Wouivre* has been personified in different ways, which are simply poetic images. It is the name our ancestors gave at the same time to snakes that glide on the ground and, by extension, to rivers that 'snake', such as the *Wouivre*, and to currents that 'snake' through the ground. Today we call these 'telluric'. Some of them spring from the movement of subterranean waters; others from faults which have brought soils of different kinds into contact, which develop differences of potential according to changes of temperature; some, again, flow from the depths of the terrestrial magma.

These currents are a manifestation of a life that goes on deep in Earth herself and where they fail to reach, the soil is dead, without fecundity, as a part of the human body would be were it no longer irrigated by the blood-stream. Contrary-wise, they carry to those places where they are found a fresh supply of life which makes the earth fruitful. These are places which the 'snakes' seek as it were of their own will, whence perhaps this likening of the currents with the serpents they symbolise.

What is more, and doubtless by way of analogy, the ancients gave the name *'Wouivres'* to the currents that today we term cosmic, or at least magnetic. They represented them by winged serpents and sometimes birds: the 'sirens' (often shewn as birds with women's faces). Places where telluric and aerial currents met and by their very nature, gave birth to flying dragons and such: the 'Mélusines', or women that are half snake.

Among the terrestrial currents some were good, some bad. The good were those which gave, and still give, health to plant, animal and man. In old days people gathered to live in these beneficent neighbourhoods: vegetation did better there, animals prospered, men enjoyed better health. The places where they were especially active were marked with stones which in some manner localised and condensed them. Sometimes tall stones were used to collect celestial currents as well; today we call them *menhirs*. These were fertility-stones, for they accumulated the fertilising properties of earth and sky.

That no-one may be under any misapprehension, let us say that the stones we are talking about were stones of utilitarian character; 'functional' stones our technocrats would call them. It is really impossible to imagine that the men of the past would have reasoned like the housewife who arranges her sitting-room and hangs a picture because 'it looks well' that way. It was certainly not because it 'looked well there' that the ancients set up a menhir. When they transported and erected the stone this was because it was useful, to fertilise the fields or for some other purpose. The same goes for dolmens. It was not for aesthetic reasons that the dolmen at Antequera, thirty metres long and wide in proportion, was carried from one place to another . . . a thing we should not know how to do today. But a dolmen is not a fertility-stone; its significance is religious. It is placed on a spot where the telluric current exercises a spiritual action on man, a spot where 'the spirit breathes'. It re-animates the cavern and it is in the bosom of Earth herself, within the dolmenic chamber, that man seeks Earth's gift.

Among all the sacred places, marked by dolmens or temples, one was held in higher repute than all others. It was situated in the country of the Carnutes . . .

And now we must go far back to the days when history is legend, symbol, allegory; yet not so far that we shall not see history written in the soil in names that resist all disorders, wars, changes.

In those times long past, the Great God of the Gauls, One and unknowable, was called by the name Belen because the sun in its precessional course found itself at the spring equinox in the constellation of the Ram, which in Gallic, preserved in old French, is 'bélin'.

Two thousand years before it was symbolically represented by the Bull, for it was through the constellation Taurus that the sun was moving at the spring equinox (in Egypt this was the bull Apis and in Ireland the Red Bull of Cualnge). When after two thousand years of the Ram the equinoctial passage went through Pisces, the Ram or Pascal Lamb was slain and Christ, God of the new age, had the Fish for hieroglyph.

In the time of Belen (from about two thousand years before Jesus Christ until the present era) places consecrated to him were called Belen's lands, Belengaard, whence all the Bellegarde, which have no connexion with either beauty or defence, Blenes, Bléneau, Balin and so on, which survive in the names of our villages and in place-names.

As was right, Belen was pledged to a consort, wife and sister, who was his material manifestation, his terrestrial and prolific aspect, Bélisama. Here we approach the heart of our problem. The Gauls consecrated to this goddess – we are not using this word in its Latin signification – a region named after her, which with the help of phonetic changes, passed successively from Bélisame to Bélisa, Belsa Biausa and finally Beauce which Suger, in his life of Louis

VI Le Gros, still calls 'The Land of Saints'.

Les Vrayes Chroniques, which preceded Rabelais' Pantagruel, relate that Bélisama, under the name of Carmelle, 'stone-bearer', virgin made fruitful by the divine spirit of Belen, brought forth a son who was a 'Son of the Giant Stone', of the stone *gante*. Stone is Gar; the being is Tua (Tuata in the plural): the son of the *pierre gante* is thus *Gar-gant-tua*. In the plural: this would have given Gargantuata, the tribe of giant stones; just as we have *Nantuata*, the *Nantuates*; people of the river, the Nant. The word is preserved in Nantua.

The good giant Gargantua, mounted on Belen's horse, Beliard (the Bayard of legend, retold by the monks of Stavelot, authors of the Exploits of the four brothers Aymon), travelled the world, like Apollo in his chariot, from east to west, following the rhythm of the seasons, clearing forests, drying up marshes, making fishponds and lakes. If we may believe Rabelais, it was he who cleared La Beauce; he or at any rate his horse that by swishing its tail razed the oak forests that covered it. And Gargantua, who occupied himself so much with the fertility of the earth, was a great mover of giant stones, quoits, perrons, menhirs, all without doubt fertility-stones.

Among these there was one, in the region consecrated to Bélisama in Suger's Land of Saints, a stone so sacred that a whole people had been commissioned with its protection. They were known as 'Guardians of the Stone', the Carnutes. And their holy place, where the stone was to be seen, was *Carnute-Is*, now Chartres, in Beauce, l'*Is of the Carnutes*.

Latinists, who claim to derive the French language from who knows what low Latin of the legionaries, explain that the names of tribes became the names of towns through an ablative form of the word. Thus, for Albert Dauzat Paris is simply *civitas de Parisiis*; but in this case and according to this fairy-tale, of what word is the town Is, Is that was swallowed up, Is the holy town which the Ismii guarded, the ablative form? And that other Is, on the Tille, near Dijon? Let us wear mourning for the Latin ablative. *Is* is not Latin, it is not even specifically Gallic. *Is* is the sacred, the sacred thing, the sacred place. One comes on it in connexion with sacred rivers, *Is-aar, Is-e*re, waters that are taboo. Amiens is not the *civitas de Ambioniis*; it is *Ambion-Is*, the *Is*, the sacred place, of the Ambions. Sens is not the *civitas de Senoniis* but *Senon-Is*, the *Is*, the sacred place, of the Senones. Chartres is not the *civitas de Carnutiis*; it is *Carnut-Is*, sacred place of the Carnutes.

In point of fact, it was not originally a town or city but simply a sacred place whose name, towards the third century, so it would appear, the town took to itself by extension. This is perfectly clear, as it is perfectly clear that the sacred stone of Bélisama was laid in the sacred place, this stone of which the Carnutes were the guardians. And this stone, brought here and set up in the night of time, is still to be seen. The cathedral was built over it.

There are proofs. In the sixteenth century a witness saw this 'vestige of the ancient altars set up to idols'. It is still there. In fact it is a dolmen. First of all because the 'druidic' grotto beneath the 'altar set up to idols' makes it a dolmenic chamber. It is here that the Black Virgin was found.

Again, there is a well, Celtic, rectangular, with the necessary machinery — it was discovered and uncovered in 1904 by René Merlet — and the dolmenic arrangements always included a well of this kind. The druids practised a form of water-baptism, which is classic in every ritual of initiation.

The well of Chartres seems to have had special importance, either because its water had special qualities or because it was thought to exercise magic power. It is thirty-three metres deep and the water-table lies about thirty metres beneath the crypt. The importance of this well for the builders of the cathedral is attested by its representation, at the north portico at the feet of Saint Modeste.

Regarding the religious significance of the place, history gives us the necessary sidelight. In his commentaries on the Gallic war, Julius Caesar, the soldier who when he was not preoccupied with his career occasionally took time to interest himself in various matters, says somewhere that the Druids had a meeting-place in some part of the Carnute forest. Traces of the forest that surrounded Chartres are still to be seen. And where would you find a place more sacred than the sacred Mound, in holy Is, in the midst of sacred forests in Bélisama's country?

I know that numerous historians, among them Julian, would place the spot on the borders of Carnute territory, on the banks of the Loire, towards Saint-Benoit-sur-Loire. But this was the *political* meeting-place of the Gallic chiefs, or of the Gauls; it was there that problems common to all the Gauls were debated and where the Druids, for this was one of their functions, arbitrated.

Besides, this region was not within Carnute territory. It was at the junction of the Senones, Eduens, Bituriges and Carnutes. It must have been at the spot that today is called Lion-en-Sulias; Lion, a Lugdunum, a fortress of Lug, patron of engineers. It is not part of the Land of the Saints.

Here is what Suchet, historian of the Cathedral, says. 'If one considers its situation, it stands at the highest part of the town, on an elevation where according to our ancient records, there was once a sacred wood in which the Druids gathered to make their sacrifices and devotions.'

'There', says Bulteau, another historian, 'was the Druids' sanctuary of sanctuaries and the seat of the sovereign tribunal. There we are in the very midst of the Gauls and the great Némète. In a word, it was the centre of Druidism.'

One more proof, which makes the Mound the meeting-point of a druidical college: the rising ground on which Chartres stands was called Place of the strong Saints; but earlier, simply Place of the Strong, which has the particular

meaning of 'Initiates'. And what was it other than this, in
the time of the Druids?

There are some amusing coincidences. Julian mentions
a dolmen, near Fontevrault, which he considers a model, in
some sort, of this kind of structure. It is 10.40 metres long
and 6.45 metres wide. Quite a morsel, which must weigh
more than one hundred tons! It is carved in the proportions of the Golden Number. And it is situated on the
territory of the commune of Saint-Fort!

Other proofs accumulate to support the ancient
importance of this Mound: various extant monuments and
above all the toponymy of the region. Were all recollection
of the Mound, the pilgrimage and the Black Virgin to be
lost, the circle of place-names that surround Chartres
would suffice to describe this holy place of the Gauls, as it
is still one of the holy places of Christianity.

There was around Chartres in the past an enormous
number of megaliths, menhirs, dolmens and other stone
structures which are called *murgers* in France, cor-
responding with the British *cairns*. Many have disappeared,
but their names remain. To give but a few examples, there
is to the south, at Morancez, a dolmen called *The Stone
that Turns*. Another in the south-east, between Berchère-
les-Pierres — whence came the stones of the cathedral —
and Sour, one of the most important Templar commands
in France, is known as *The Crumpled Stone*. Near by, are
two places named *The Covered Stone* whose dolmens have
disappeared. Or are still buried.

To the south-east, nearer Chartres, is a place-name
Beaulieu, which is a *Lieu-Belen* (south of the Loire it
would have been *Bellac*), near the *Beaumonts*, which are
Belen-mons.

To the east we have The Murgers, near *Nogent-le-Phaye*,
which is a *Nogent-la-Fée*; further east still, *Archevilliers*,
with a place named *L'Arche*; and this *arche* or ark comes
from *Arca*, ligurian and gallic for dolmen.

Northward there is a village called *Gorget*, under which

name one would soon perceive a *Lieu-Gargan*. Quite close to this, north-west, is a *Butte Celtique*, or Celtic Mound, whose name seems to me recent; but it is near a menhir called *The Fairy's Foot*, a place named *The White Ladies*, and another *The Stony Fields*, where without doubt there once were sacred stones that have disappeared.

It is then reasonable to declare that none of this is a matter of chance.

If the Druids gathered here; if men accepted the discomforts and dangers of pilgrimage; it was because they knew they would find in this place a 'spirit', to use an expression of Barrès, a 'spirit' particularly powerful and of rare quality. If you prefer it in modern terms, let us say that this Mound on which the cathedral stands is a place where a particular telluric current comes to a head. There was a bishop of Chartres, not one of those who smashed stained-glass windows to get more light or who filled the cathedral with loudspeakers, Monseigneur Pie, who said of his church that 'It's source is below and above.'

To make use of an image which the Christian icono-graphers applied to thousands of examples — not that it is certain they always knew what they were about — the feet of Notre-Dame, the Virgin, are on the head of the snake, the *Wouivre*.

The source is certainly down below and this is the reason why the dolmen was erected in this spot; likewise the various churches that have succeeded one another here. And one sees why canon Bulteau wrote: 'One can say that Chartres is the classic place of the Incarnation in the West.'

This is what explains the allegory of the Black Virgin: Mother Earth giving birth, without any other intervention but that of Heaven — we will call it 'cosmic' — to a manifestation, an active radiation whose quality may be called divine.

Examination of the situation of Chartres in France as a whole reveals yet another curious thing. There exists in what

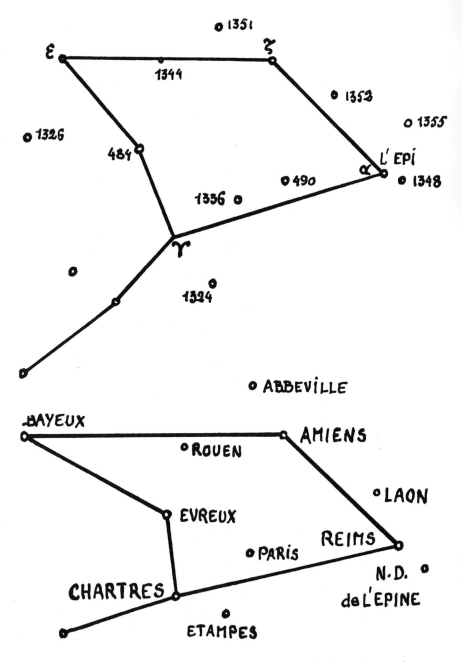

The constellation of Virgo and the pattern of Notre Dames in France.

was Belgian Gaul, in the old provinces of Champagne, Picardy, Ile-de-France and Neustrie, a certain number of XIIth and XIIIth century cathedrals, bearing the name of Notre-Dame, which reproduce, taken together, on Earth the constellation of the Virgin as seen in the sky. If one relates the stars with the towns in which these cathedrals stand, l'*Epi de la Vierge* would be Reims; *Gamma,* Chartres; *Zeta* Amiens; *Epsilon,* Bayeux. Among the smaller stars we find Evreux, Etampes, Laon, all of these having a Notre-Dame of the best period. One even finds, in the place of one of the smaller stars, near l'*Epi,* a Notre-Dame-de-l'Epine, which was built much later, but its building opens a mystery.

Maurice Leblanc had already noted, before others, that the Benedictine Abbeys of the Caux country trace on Earth the form of the Great Bear. It has recently been discovered that the fields which surround Glastonbury, in Somerset (where the Isle of Avalon is traditionally said to have been, with the Druidic well of the Grail: Chalice Well and Arthur's Tomb) befigure the twelve signs of the Zodiac. One may perfectly well ask if these correspondences between Earth and Heaven are the work of human fantasy, or if they were dictated by some kind of higher necessity, working in men who obeyed a sort of cosmic instinct.

However this may be, as far as Chartres is concerned we have all the data of the problem; I would rather say, the pilgrimage.

The currents in old Earth are numerous and various; but here, in Chartres, we are concerned with one that is especially sacred, capable of awakening a man to the spiritual life. The *Divine* is born here and no material influence may be allowed to trouble or destroy it. The Hill of Chartres must not be polluted. That is why among all the French cathedrals Chartres is the only one in which no king, cardinal or bishop is interred. The Hill must remain virgin.

The bishops of Chartres have their tombs under the chapel of Saint Piat which was built at the extremity of the XIVth century apse outside the sacred Mound. The canons were buried at the end of the apse, in a small cemetery, now unused, likewise beyond the sacred ground.

And the taboo placed on the Mound must be extremely powerful, since, even in our time when everything is overturned without thought, there has been no digging on the ground which the pillars of choir and nave enclose.

3 A Mysterious Orientation

The choice of the Mound was not a matter of chance. Chartres is a place where spirit pervades, or can pervade, matter; a place where spirit incarnates, more especially at the time of the great pulsations of the *Wouivre,* seasonal pulsations, analogous to those of the blood-stream, which govern the dates of pilgrimage. It is then that initiation may perhaps be received. A high initiation, since the Druids made use of it for themselves. And do not let there be misunderstanding. When I speak of initiation I am not speaking of mere instruction or learning. Initiation is not a degree of knowledge, but a *state.* It is, or was until the term was debased by haphazard use in the sacristies, what the early Christians understood by a *state of grace.* One can be in a state of grace while completely ignorant of the metric system and know nothing about theology. One can be in a state of grace and perfectly amoral.

To be initiated is to be introduced; to be integrated with the play of natural forces, to understand them, receive them into oneself — the etymology of the word is perfectly clear — it is to experience them, as though by a higher instinct in which the brain plays no part. It is to be reunited and linked with them; thus, to be religious in the proper sense of the word (Latin, religare, to rebind). In a word, it is to be penetrated and imbued by Spirit.

Now at Chartres, as at some other places, as for instance Puy-en-Velay or Saint-Jacques-de-Compostella, the Earth has a particular quality, a telluric current of special power which enables a man to obtain such integration, initiation, grace; and this new birth into a higher state of humanity must have been held in the highest esteem to set such crowds of pilgrims on the road. Admittedly, among all those who were called, the number of chosen must have been very small and no doubt the Druids, who were for a long time the hierophants of the place, took care only to initiate those worthy of it who, from this very fact would not be tempted to make evil use of powers that were the evident result.

Indeed, it seems likely that in the beginning the pilgrimage was only made by an élite who came seeking a final consecration, that of the 'new birth'.

Though in a manner very confused, tradition has preserved the memory of the 'periplus', in which the elements of initiation were given piecemeal in one holy place after another until the new birth itself was achieved. Thus, we know, the Druids acted; thus also the travelling philosophers of Greece, for whom it was an obligation to visit the Egyptian temples. There must have been, as in the Game of the Goose or Hopscotch, in which children hopping on one leg propel a quoit through a succession of compartments, a set course; the results obtained in one determining what should happen in another. Later, crowds followed; but it is hardly in doubt that they did not long have a claim to anything but an imitation; certainly not to the experience of three rebirths in the covered passage that *must* have led to the dolmen and *must* have had the same orientation as the cathedral.

There is in Chartres, on the banks of the Eure, almost on the axis of the cathedral, high and dominant on its Mound, a small disused romanesque church, very simple and in pure style, whose special feature at one time was that its choir was built on an arch thrown out over the river as if to steep itself in the spirit of running water. The arch is now broken; only some vestiges remain. The church

It seems that the image-maker who sculpted the tympanum of the door of The Nativity at the royal entrance to Chartres Cathedral took for his model the Black Virgin from the crypt, which was destroyed in the sixteenth-century. (Chapter 2.) *Photo: Giraudon.*

The church of Saint Andrew, Chartres used to have its choir on an arch, now vanished, over the River Eure. (Chapter 3.)

The Celtic well at the foot of Sainte Modeste (North Door). (Chapter 2.)

The vault of Chartres. *Photo: Jean Roubier.*

Aerial view of the cathedral showing towers, transepts and nave. (Chapter 5.)

Buttresses of north transept the nave, and 'tours de blocag the trans (Chapter 5.)

←

Aspiration stone ... li strength of cathedral. Age Rapho.

Two sirens drinking from the Grail cup. (Inner capital of the North tower.) (Chapter 14.) *Archives photographiques.*

Near: Moses between Abraham and Samuel, carrying, with the Tables of the Law, the column of the Temple surmounted by a winged serpent (North door). (Chapter 12.) *Photo: Giraudon.*

Middle: Saint Loup. On the Capital is represented the little scene of the materialization of the emerald in the calyx. (Saint Loup de Naud.) (Chapter 14.) *Photo: Jean Roubier.*

Right: Melchisedek bearing the Grail cup out of which ccmes the Stone. (Chapter 14.) *Photo: Giraudon.*

The passage of the Ark, casket on wheels . . . On the right-hand column a scene (very damaged) of massacre. Some personage is taking hold of the Ark, with a cloth in his hand. (Chapter 9.)

must have served for a long time as a granary or warehouse. The Historic Monuments people, who have done what they could for several years to restore the church, have accumulated plenty of old stones that are not without interest.

It is possible that the church's situation, slightly to the north of the axis of the cathedral, may be the result of chance; but this would be astonishing when one remembers what care the ancients, including Christians, took to establish their cult-sites over points that were tellurically potent — that is, on holy ground. Does not this situation awaken a sense of the telluric current, the Wouivre that bathes Notre-Dame with its terrestrial emanations?

For unlike most Christian churches of old days, the head of this cathedral is directed, not to the east but the north-east, by more than 45°, or exactly, if one may accept the diagrams and alignments given by the National Geographical Institute, 47°. If some modern church were under discussion this would be without interest, but Chartres is not a modern church and this detail regarding the inclination of its axis is very important indeed. Once again we must go far back and link the particular case of Chartres with some kind of general law.

Earth turns from West to East, which is why the fixed stars seem by reference to Earth to turn from East to West; sun and stars . . .

Earth turns with its aerial envelope; but there is another and invisible thing that does not turn with her, not at the same time that is, the medium in which the worlds swim. The Greeks called this *Aether*; the alchemists *Spirit of the World*; our ancestors the *Winged Wouivre*, the celestial *Great Serpent*, this because of a certain qualitative analogy with the subterranean Wouivres. This ether in which we move, supposed, I say supposed, to be immobile, is animated, by reference to ourselves, by a movement contrary to our own, East to West.

Useless, I presume, to specify that we are talking about a vital current, as necessary to life as no matter what other element, water or air, earth or fire. It seems, what is more, to exert an action that is not negligible on the evolution of things and being.

In this current man, who makes use of it unknown to himself, may take two attitudes, two possible positions, just as if it were a river of water: he may face it or let himself be carried along.

Here is a little experiment, well enough known. Thrust a knitting needle through an apple or orange; place an ant on the fruit and turn the fruit round and round: the ant will move in the direction contrary to the direction of rotation, that is, westward . . . demanding the least effort no doubt. And thus, on Earth, do human migrations; for man in the mass acts as if the mass had no other instinct than the animal. Towns, it is known, move westward.

But man, when he gets to a certain stage of individuality, does not stand back to the stream; he faces it, meets it, the better to soak himself in it and receive its inestimable gift. He may even open his arms to it in the attitude of a man at prayer. It was thus, until lately, that a priest stood at the altar; must indeed do so, facing the east; thus also the faithful, on their feet and with feet bare, so as to unite in themselves the current that derives from the earth with that which derives from the sky. To turn the back is to refuse the gift, to refuse what is life-giving. The mythical lands of the dead always lie westward, whether the Egyptian Lands of the Dead or the Isle of Avalon (A-val) of the Celts.

This is why churches have always been oriented in the literal sense of the term. Why then is Chartres turned not to the East but to the North-East? A mistake of the builder's? Impossible. He would have been the only one in all Christendom to have 'lost the north point'.

There is but one explanation — the direction of the

telluric current. One goes to Chartres to ask something of Earth and one must bathe in the terrestrial current, face towards it. This it is that allows us to suppose, with every appearance of total truth, that at the time when the religious monument of the sacred Mound was a dolmen, access to it must have been by a covered way through which a man went, bathed in the telluric current, to the new birth which is impregnation of his being with divine Spirit.

Over and above this, it is truly remarkable that the Christians should have reconstituted this 'covered way', for what otherwise are the galleries that lead from the towers of the façade to the grotto where Our-Lady-of-Under-the-Earth was found, to the site of the dolmen, the well whose water was reputed miraculous long before?

4 An Instrument of Music

Chartres is a gothic monument.

Gothic architecture is a system of building that rests on what is called the ogive.

The appearance of this style is generally dated around the year 1130 A.D. According to Régine Pernoud, it was in Lombardy that the earliest known pointed arches appeared; also in the Alpine region and in the Midi*. Jean Taralon has discovered some just as early at Jumieges† and examples have been noted in England.

In a word, one does not know. Gothic appeared everywhere at the same time in the Christian west; always in the Benedictine or Cistercian abbeys, Cistercian above all.

Another thing. Gothic appeared after the first Crusade and more particularly after the return in 1128 of the first nine Knights Templar. Twelve years after this date, Suger, Abbot of Saint-Denis, erected a gothic vault on the romanesque foundations of his abbey. The cathedral at Noyon was begun at about the same time. And from now on churches, abbey or lay, were built in this style; above all in the Ile-de-France and in Champagne.

The fact is remarkable enough for us to take note of it, because it indicates that the master-builders were trained and there must therefore have been a *school* from which

* Régine Pernoud: les Grandes Époques de l'Art en Occident, Éditions de Chêne, 1954.
† Jean Taralon: Jumiéges. Éditions du Cert, 1962.

they spread over the Christian west; and because it assumes a *will* to make this method of building widely employed. Which implies that those who promoted the movement, men of religion, expected of this ogival device a potent religious effect. Thus, the story of the gothic development poses the whole of the gothic mystery.

The gothic does not follow the romanesque. They existed together. The romanesque builders carried on with their romanesque while the gothic builders erected their gothic. And the two 'schools' did not mix. When the romanesque school tried its hand at gothic there only resulted, most of the time, a somewhat bastard style which was named, later, and with courtesy, 'transitional'. The gothic builders themselves did not grope. The builders of Senlis, in 1154, knew exactly what they were about.

It is known that the builders of churches were united in fraternities. We are concerned with two such, different (and this is important), since they were not unaware of one another. For the rest, the necessary science in the one and the other was not the same, though both systems sprang from the same desire, namely, to make use of Earth-Mother's gift, the telluric current at a given place, in the interest of mankind.

The simplest, and first, thing was evidently to trace these currents to their source, in Earth herself, in the cavern; or again by usage of the water that was impregnated with it; whence the ritual well. Where there was no cavern, or if it was unsuitable, they made an artificial one which, for the Megalithics, was the dolmenic chamber, for Christians the crypt.

To reinforce the current's action, the Megalithic builders had recourse to a remarkable stone instrument, the dolmen. Apart from other qualities stone has two that are very striking. First, like its little artificial sister the brick it is an accumulator; it becomes charged with telluric or cosmic 'influences'. Second, it is capable of vibration. One can conceive of a musical instrument made of stones, carved in the right proportions (like obelisks). Now the remarkable instrument which is a dolmen, a stone table resting on two, three or four supports, rather resembles the metal strip of a Xylophone. The table, submitted to two contrary forces, its cohesiveness and its weight, is thus in a state of tension and is susceptible of vibration like the stretched piano-string. It is at the same time an accumulator and an amplifier. Thus, the potency of the telluric wave attains its maximum force in the dolmenic chamber, which acts like a resonant drum. This supposes, it will be said, a higher degree of science than one can ascribe to hunters of bison who shaped their arrows out of flints. But it would also be absurd to imagine that dolmens were erected on behalf of folklore, or the cathedral to embellish the countryside of La Beauce.

And what do we know about the knowledge of these 'savages' who among the mountains of Andalusia transported a little dolmen nearly thirty metres long and wide in proportion, a thing modern machines would hardly succeed in doing? However this may be, when the art and science of moving and erecting these enormous stone tables disappeared other methods were tried.

It was no doubt for want of the necessary knowledge that first primitive Christianity, then the Byzantines and the Romans constructed, above ground, a resonance chamber, the original cave, utilising cupola and concave vault, heritage of Rome. But such a vault, static, heavy but without tension, is incapable of vibration. And this led the Benedictine abbeys to step up the terrestrial action on the one hand with sound – to which we owe Gregorian music – and on the other with that visual music that constitutes the geometrical harmony of monumental proportions and forms.

Towards the end of the eleventh century, without doubt

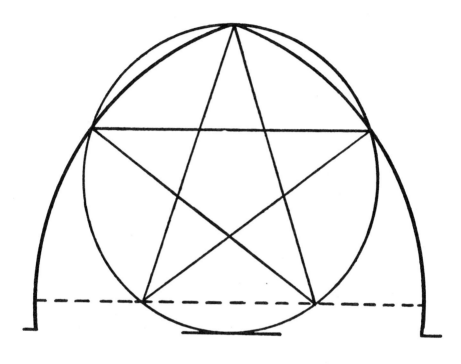

Based on the five-pointed star, traditional symbol of Man.

later than the Persians, Cluny, it would seem, discovered the ogive and its properties. The discovery was capital. The physical and physiological action of the ogive on man is extraordinary. Whether it is due to mimesis, to the action of lines of force or to other causes, the ogive *works* on mankind. Beneath it, a man pulls himself together, stands upright. It is very important historically. It dates the beginning of an individual consciousness among men, until then reduced to a condition of total slavery by the 'race of seigneurs'. The idea of a community, a common people, dates from it.

This is yet more important in a religious sense, because physiologically telluric or other currents can only enter man *via* a vertebral column that is straight and vertical. Men can only move to a higher state by standing upright.

This human quality of the ogive was so well known to the builders of that time that in the romanesque Basilica at Vézelay they built a sort of immense ogival gable on top of the roman porch which they were unwilling, or unable, to destroy — it answers no kind of architectural necessity. We meet it again in the shape and proportions of the ogive at Chartres, not that of the main entrance or west doorway, which would no doubt repay analysis, but that of the crossed ogives of the vault. This again is based on the traditional symbol of man, the five-pointed star.

This star is enclosed in a circle whose diameter is the height of the keystone of the vault. The two lower points of the star are at the centre of arcs of a circle which form the two sides of the ogive. The arcs cut the circle at two higher lateral points. The keystone of the vault is at the highest point of the star.

Is the inclusion of man in the vault merely symbolic? Even if so, is the symbol without direct action on man himself? It is hardly likely that it was without any thought of such action that the master-builder made this vault an extension of mankind himself, integrated with the general harmony of the building.

From the ogive the 'creators' of gothic went on to derive much more by a process of 'crossing' it. They found the high secret of the musical stone, the stone under tension, a secret lost when men lost the science of transporting the huge dolmen-tables.

The crossed ogive is built on the principle of the transformation of lateral into vertical thrust. It is a sum of forces in which the vault no longer weighs down but springs upward under the lateral counterthrust of buttresses. If it is to last, the gothic monument requires perfect adjustment between weight and thrust; the weight that creates the thrust becomes itself its own negation. The activity in the stone is therefore in a state of constant tension which the art of the master-builder can 'tune' like a harp-string. For a gothic cathedral is not only a musical instrument by similitude.

(Evidently this refutes an official evolutionism that sees in the gothic a sort of development of the romanesque, simpler and less costly to build. In fact the two systems are antipodal to each other. The romanesque, essentially static, handles forces that are directed downward; the vault weighs on the walls. The gothic, built up on a dynamic of pressures, handles forces directed upwards. The romanesque vault collapses; the gothic leaps. No doubt one can find them blended in a particular monument, but never in the vault. Romanesque foundations and walls have served to uphold gothic lancets and builders have not neglected to make use when they could of massive romanesque buttresses as supports, to preserve romanesque walls and windows; but that does not in the least imply that the one style passes into the other by evolutionary stages.)

But why the term 'gothic'? There is nothing 'gothic' in these buildings which, strangely enough, only reached their full development within the limits of the Celtic world.

Plenty of etymologies have been proposed. Three of them seem useful.

(i) *A Celtic etymology.* In Celtic, *Ar-Goat* is wooded country, a country of trees; not only does gothic sometimes wear the appearance of forests of high trees mingling their foliage, but before becoming a job for stone-cutters and masons the gothic monument was the work of carpenters. The gothic vault, drawn on the ground and prefabricated, was put up on calibrated stages. Without carpenters, without wood, no vault resting on crossed ogives. It is a *goatique* art.

(ii) *A Greek etymology.* Gothic derived from goètie: magic from the Greek *Goes*: compare sorcier, goétis; sortilège, goétéou, to fascinate. It is an art of *envoûtement* or spell-casting – the term is direct. There could be much to say on this *envoûtement,* this envolutement, this putting under a vault; this passage from the upright to the curve, from a linear, terrestrial geometry to a curved or cosmic geometry. Let us confine ourselves to the idea of magical action, a *goetic* art.

(iii) *A Cabbalistic etymology.* This is given by the scholar Adept *Fulcanelli* in 'Le Mystère des Cathédrales',* where he derives gothic art from *argotique,* from the ship *Argo*; *argotique* being primitively a secret, cabbalistic, alchemical language. Here we have an aspect of occult knowledge built into the cathedral; an aspect of hermetic science that makes the cathedral a crucible for human transmutation.

As often happens, the three etymologies overlap and are exact.

A cathedral is built *goatiquement,* not only according to the qualities of wood but also according to the rules governing vegetable growth. It is built *goétiquement,* to act magically on man and according to harmonic laws whose action is obvious. It is built *argotiquement,* according to

---

* Fulcanelli: *Le Mystère des Cathédrales. Pauvert. 1964.*

'religious' laws that make it the finest vessel of escape into 'the beyond' ever constructed.

We shall come across these three aspects again in connection with the *three tables* from which the proportions and dimensions of the cathedral at Chartres derive.

5 An Astonishing Science

The gothic style sprang fully armed from heads that had astonishing knowledge in them.

In order to achieve the gothic vault and all that goes with it, it was necessary, seven hundred years before Monge, to discover nothing less than a descriptive geometry capable of shewing in a simple outline drawn on the ground not only the relationships of volume, upright and curve, but the whole play of thrust and counterthrust through the action of harmonic geometrical forces.

This science, which is not lost, was imparted, at least in its material aspect, to religious builders by the monks of Citeaux; 'missionaries of the gothic' as Pierre de Colombier called them. The builders of those distant days passed it on to the apprentices in their brotherhoods or guilds. In this way it came down to our own times and is still taught in the 'canteens' of their successors the Companions of Duty. They make no mystery of this. They make no mystery of its origin, but the secret is strictly kept like the secret of other traditional teachings.

They were known, last century, under the name of 'Companions of the Tour of France'. It was to them that Eiffel appealed for the building of his tower and Viollet-le-Duc for his restorations. Whatever may have been their beliefs, they kept alive a quasi-religious conception and philosophy of labour in absolute respect for the person and for human liberty. This is perfectly in line with the gothic conception, which is to provide men with a rational means of evolution towards greater fullness in themselves. The ogive of the great west door is the most conclusive example.

In romanesque architecture there is always a narthex at public entrances; a place where you halt, wait, recollect yourself; a place of purification, but a purification that a man must effect in himself. With effort. The narthex disappeared with the arrival of the gothic style, for now the ogive of the great entrance did the work of purification. The ogive makes a man stand erect and by this means alone makes him conscious of himself. It is no longer a sheep that enters the church but, whether he is good or bad, a man. Evolution has begun.

Mechanically. It will go on, as we shall see, within him, until it produces if not consciousness at least a certain cosmic awareness which is itself an awakening.

But let us not deceive ourselves. A cathedral is for the people, one is inclined to say for the 'laity'; it is for the public and not for those who of their own will are seeking to attain a certain condition. Saint Bernard deals very concisely with this in his famous letter to the Venerable Peter. 'Art is only a means, useful only to the simple and ignorant, useless and even harmful to the wise and perfect. Consequently, monks should leave the care of architecture to pastors whose duty lies among the people.'

It has been supposed that he rejected art. What a mistake, since it was his own Order that was to propagate and teach the gothic system and, if we are to believe Mlle Anne-Marie Armand, he was himself the creator of the gothic cathedral in its profoundest significance. And it is true that there are certain puzzling coincidences between Saint Bernard's toings and froings and the putting of work in hand at the stoneyards.

But what knowledge must they have had, these creators and builders, to achieve the realisation, at this stage, of such instruments of action?

One can easily see that this pile of stone so taut, according to Claudel, 'that you could make it ring with a fingernail', is a replica of the dolmen and imitates its use of the telluric currents. And as in the dolmen the edifice is connected with water through the well that existed originally at the level of the choir in every cathedral.

But there is more than this to a cathedral. It lifts itself into the air. It plunges — and for this cause it is made very high — in aerial currents, rain from the sky, atmospheric storms, the great cosmic streams. It gathers, absorbs and transmits light. Earth, water, air and fire! What better crucible has there ever been for the finest of human alchemies?

For it is certainly a question of alchemy; the transmutation, not of metal, but of man. Of man, whom it is wished to lead to a higher state of humanity. But that it may be effective, the instrument must be adapted to Earth, Heaven and Man himself. In those obscure times — and they were that — whence could the knowledge come?

The Grand Master of the Templars carried an abacus, the master-builder's staff.

6 The Mission of the Nine Knights Templar

History tells us that in the year 1118 nine French knights, devout, religious and believing in God, presented themselves before the king of Jerusalem Baldwin II and explained that they planned to form themselves into a company with a view to protecting pilgrims from robbers and murderers and to policing the public highways.

The king received them courteously and accepted their proposal. He gave them by way of lodging a house he possessed in a wing of his palace, on the site of the old Temple of Solomon, in the Masjid-el-Aksa.

Next, the nine knights visited the Patriarch to inform him of the charge they had taken on themselves and of their wish to be considered 'Soldiers of Christ' and to live in monastic fashion — or semi-monastic, for they remained laymen until 1128. The Patriarch having approved, they made between his hands the three vows of chastity, obedience and non-possession of personal property. (The term William de Tyr uses is *sine proprio*, which was translated, a bit too soon, into poverty.)

Finally, the canons of Saint-Sepulchre handed over to them, on certain conditions, a piece of ground surrounding the house that had been lent them by the king.

History tells us likewise that because of the house they occupied on the site of Solomon's Temple they were given the name of Knights of the Temple or Templars. This was the result of a singular premonition.

Thus arose the legend of the Order of Templars which was to leave its mark on Christianity. It reaches its end with the burning of the last Grand Master, Jacques de Molay, at the stake in 1314 by Philippe le Bel.

These, it was said, were *poor* knights. Their leader was *Hughes de Payns* who became first Grand Master when the Order was constituted. He held a fief to the north-west of Troyes, which became the first command-in-chief in the West. He was related to the counts of Champagne.

His second-in-command was *Godefroy de Saint-Omer*, a Fleming. It was certainly to one of his relatives that Baldwin I entrusted Tiberias and the principality of Galilee.

Another was *André de Montbard*, uncle of Saint Bernard, Abbot of Clairvaux. It is known that he was related to the Counts of Burgundy.

Payen de Montdidier and *Archambaud de Saint-Amand* were both Flemish.

As to the rest, only the patronymics or only the Christian names are known: *Gondemare, Rosal, Godefroy* and *Geoffroy Bisol.* But all this adds up to a somewhat relative poverty. Let us admit that they were poor, that their squires were poor, that their men-at-arms and their servants were poor. For they had servants with them of necessity. In those days a knight could not arm himself without help nor fight by himself.

It is none the less probable that they kept their vow not to hold personal possessions; and this vow was respected throughout the history of the Templars, whatever the wealth of the Order.

The vow of chastity must also be observed. It is likely that this corresponds with an ideal prevalent in those times regarding a company of knights eager to assure the salvation of their souls; but the sacrifice was small in relation to the mission to police the pilgrim routes which they assigned themselves. In such work one bawdy soldier is worth as much as one blameless knight.

The task was indeed meritorious and useful. Besides raids by armed Mussulmen, the back-country between Jaffa and Jerusalem was infested with brigand Bedouins who plundered the pilgrims, a game in which the native, honest Christian lent a willing hand.

Nevertheless, did not this watching of the highways overlap with a mission that another Order assigned to itself, an Order already in being although not yet altogether an Order of Chivalry? Its task was to lodge the pilgrims *and defend them*: This was the Order of Hospitallers of Saint John of Jerusalem. Logic, as well as sound organisation, would have required that these nine Knights who wished to defend the pilgrims should have addressed themselves to the Order of Hospitallers. They did nothing of the kind.

According to the story, one has to point out, the nine knights arrived in Jerusalem in a somewhat unusual way. They were not crusaders, or they would have been part of a band of troop. They were not pilgrims: knights who came on pilgrimage, men of arms, were there to draw the sword in the name of God, not to box the ears of highwaymen. What is more, they took part in *no* warlike activity. They did not reside permanently in the Holy Land: otherwise the king would not have been obliged to afford them lodging.

They seem to have been completely independent and they at once became the object of singular benevolence on the part of the king who gave them part of his palace and turned out the canons of Saint-Sepulchre. And shortly, when the Frankish kings moved into the citadel of the Tower of David, the whole of Solomon's Temple was abandoned to the sole occupation of the nine knights.

It all happened as if it had been *willed* that they should have this place and have it to themselves. The historian Guillaume de Tyr is precise on the subject: throughout nine years they refused all company, all recruitment — except, and this is a point to note — that towards 1125 another knight, *Hugues*, Count of Champagne, abandoned his county, left wife and children, and came to join them. A sovereign ruler of France come to police roads and communications!

It would seem clear, evident to the least informed, that the nine, later ten, knights were not there to police the roads. Their ostensible mission conceals another, one that was carried out in Solomon's Temple itself, which everyone else had quitted that they might have the sole use of it.

The nine knights formed, then, what today we should call a 'commando' with a mission. They were sent there. By whom? We must recall their oath of obedience.

The Patriarch of Jerusalem had heard the vows of the nine knights, their hands between his: the vows of poverty, chastity and obedience. A question arises: obedience to whom or to what? Monks obey a rule of a superior; but in 1123 Hugues de Payns still puts his signature to a deed as a layman. There is thus no question of obedience to a rule that does not yet exist. The nine are not, officially, religious.

One does not make a vow of obedience to a king but an oath of allegiance.

It was not to the Patriarch of Jerusalem, to whom they never gave obedience.

What then? Texts will give us the answer.

There exists in the 'privileges' or 'prerogatives' of the Cistercian Order a form of oath for Knights of the Temple (which seems, moreover, to be that of the knights affiliated with them). Here it is:

'I swear to consecrate my speech, my strength and my life in defence of the belief in the unity of God and the mysteries of the Faith. I promise to submit myself and to be obedient to the Grand Master of the Order. When the Saracens invade Christendom I will go oversea to the deliverance of my brothers. I will give the help of my arm to the Church and to the Kings against the infidel Princes. As long as my foes are not more than three to one I will fight them and not take flight. Alone I will fight them if they are miscreants.'

Why should this be found among the 'privileges' of the Cistercian Order?

Here is part of the formula which the Master or Prior of the province of Portugal must subscribe, preserved in a manuscript from Alcobaca, where there is or was a Cistercian abbey.

'I, X . . . Knight of the Temple, newly elected master of the Knights that are in Portugal, promise . . . to submit myself to the Master-General of the Order, according to the statutes prescribed by our Father Saint Bernard . . . and that I will never refuse any help to the religious, chiefly the religious of Citeaux and their abbots, as being our brothers and companions . . .'

The text is clear: 'to the religious of Citeaux and their abbots, as being our *brothers* and our *companions.*' The word 'brother' could be subject to ambiguity if used to cover the entire monastic order, but there can be no ambiguity as regards the word companion. These are they who eat the same bread, who band together, who are harnessed to the same task.

But there is an even more explicit text.

In April 1310, at the time of the trial of the Templars, Brother Aymery of the diocese of Limoges, deposed before the pontifical attorneys at the abbey Saint Geneviève, in the name of the Templars, a defence in the form of a prayer which is at the same time a declaration of faith and a recalling of the Order's achievements. Addressed to God, it runs: 'Thine Order, that of the Temple, was founded in General Council in honour of the Sainted and Glorious Virgin Mary, Thy Mother, by the Blessed Bernard, Thy Holy Confessor, chosen for this office by Holy Roman Church. It is he who, with other upright men, instructed the Order and gave it its mission.'

Then, again, addressing itself to the Virgin: 'Holy Mary, Mother of God, uphold your religion (read *your Order*) which was founded by your saintly and dear confessor, the Blessed Bernard . . .'

This is clear, succinct and complete. The patron saint is Saint Bernard and the vow of obedience, before the Order was formally constituted, was made to him. And the knights were entrusted with a mission which they did not themselves invent. They obeyed.

In confirmation of this a sheaf of coincidences could reasonably be adduced by way of indirect proof.

Their head, Hugues de Payns, vassal of the Count of Champagne and related to him, was a near enough neighbour to the Cistercian Abbey of Clairvaux whose abbot was Saint Bernard. It would seem unlikely that Bernard, counsellor if not 'director' to the entire nobility of Champagne, did not know him.

André de Montbard was own uncle to Saint Bernard, brother to his mother Aleth de Montbard. When one realises what influence the abbot exercised over his own family, it is difficult to suppose that André did not at least ask Bernard's advice, a man with whom he was moreover to enter into correspondence, addressing him as his direct superior.

Later, it was the real suzerain of Clairvaux, donor of abbey lands, Hugues de Champagne, who joined the Templars in the Holy Land.

The other known knights were Flemish. Now, on the death of the king of Jerusalem, Baldwin I, the kingdom was offered to his brother Eustache de Boulogne, who set out; but when, having reached Les Pouilles, he learnt that his cousin, the Compte d'Edesse, had got himself crowned, he turned back, giving his knights permission to pursue their voyage abroad.

The route from Flanders to Italy passes through Champagne. It was therefore natural that Eustache de

Boulogne should make contact with the ruler whose land he was crossing: the Count of Champagne, Hugues, the future Templar who, what is more, was back from the Holy Land; likewise with the most remarkable religious personality of the West, Bernard de Clairvaux. Everything points, it will be seen, to the Sainted Abbot, more or less through the Count of Champagne, whose somewhat mysterious figure would seem to be closely associated with the beginnings of this story.

I find it likely, because logic will have it that way, that the three Flemish knights, Hugues de Saint Omer, Payen de Mondidier and Archambaud de Saint-Amand, formed part of Eustache de Boulogne's escort and that at any rate the two who belonged to Champagne, Hugues de Payns and André de Montbard, sent on a mission by Saint Bernard, joined it. This supposes that Eustache de Boulogne was either little or much *au courant* with the mission entrusted to the men of Champagne, which, if one reflects, seems perfectly normal: Eustache was on his way to become king of Jerusalem, therefore the man in the best position to help. But when, having reached Les Pouilles, he learnt that his cousin was already on the throne, he decided to abandon the journey and left certain of his knights to incorporate themselves in the mission of Hugues de Payns in order to help things on with the new King, Baldwin II, who was Flemish like themselves and with whom they were no doubt related.

I sometimes have the impression that all this has been told, under a veil of allegory, in the tales of the Round Table, at least in those episodes that relate specifically to the Holy Grail, where Lancelot discovers a castle in which the sacred vessel is kept but he is unable to reach it, and Galahad cannot reach the castle nor can Perceval handle· the cup. For it is with the Grail that we are in fact concerned.

7 In the Temple of Solomon

It is clear enough that Bernard de Clairvaux did not send Hugues de Payns nor his uncle André de Montbard to police the highways. Neither was it with that object that Eustache de Boulogne parted from his knights, nor why Hugues de Champagne, in 1125, abandoned his lands, which were nearly a kingdom.

But if protection of the highways was a blind, what could the real mission of the nine knights be?

They were picked knights, that is to say brave men — not only physically no doubt — trained in arms. But they are not to fight; they are to take only the smallest risk of their lives.

Their guard-duties obliged them to live in contact with the world, but it was exacted of them that they should conduct themselves like monks; that they should be chaste, dispassionate. Nothing must turn them from their duty. They are to be, not exactly poor, but without personal possessions . . . thus, it was impossible to bribe them. And above all they must give absolute obedience. Duty before all.

Clearly, if men were to accept such sacrifices their mission must have been noble and important. Besides, other things being equal, how can one help thinking of the gathering of atomic experts, towards the end of the last war, in the American desert of Los Alamos in order to construct the first atomic bomb?

The alacrity with which the Temple of Solomon was put at their disposal shews plainly enough where the key to the riddle is to be sought. Otherwise it would seem unlikely that there should have been handed over to nine knights an establishment that accommodated at the same time the King, his household and the canons of Saint Sepulchre. They were certainly afforded every comfort, these poor knights; comforts which far exceeded the needs of men whose job was to safeguard roads and communications. If the Nine wished to live by themselves, it was necessarily because they were engaged, not on the roads but in the Temple itself, in some secret activity.

What activity? It can only be a question of searching for something hidden. In fact they were about to open up Solomon's immense stables, beneath the site of the Temple, which were certainly sealed up before their arrival, for no mention of them has been found since the Temple was destroyed.

Jean de Würtzburg, German crusader, who saw the stables, describes them as follows. 'One sees a stable of such marvellous capacity and extent that it could house more than two thousand horses or fifteen hundred camels.'

Only one explanation is possible: the nine knights went there to seek, keep and take away something of such importance that the mission called for men who were above human passion; something so precious and dangerous that it must be kept in absolute secrecy.

What could be so important, sacred, precious, dangerous? Unless it was the Ark of the Covenant and the Tables of the Law?

The Ark and the Tables are not perhaps what is generally supposed. What are they then?

The Ark was a coffer made of resinous wood and covered, inside and out, with two plates of gold. Electrically speaking, it was a condenser. God was a sound electrician. So was Moses, who affixed to the condenser four metal antennae in the shape of Cherubim to accumulate enough static electricity to strike dead a man like poor Uzza who tried one day to touch this vessel. It was enough in any case to give a good shock, even to make sparks.

The Ark, then, is a coffer that ensures its own protection. It is not however merely a coffer. What is important is what it contains: the Tables of Witness or Tables of the Law.

It says in the Book of Exodus, xxxi. 18, 'And he gave unto Moses, when he had made an end of communing with him upon Mount Sinai, two tables of testimony, tables of stone, written with the finger of God.' One knows how Moses, when he came down from Sinai, found the people making sacrifice to the golden calf. Growing angry, he smashed the tables, reduced the calf to powder, spread the powder on water and made the people drink it . . . since when, mischievous tongues have said, the people have suffered an inextinguishable thirst for gold.

At last Moses' anger cooled; God's too, so that he consented to engrave fresh tables, 'written on both sides'. Which may mean on the front and on the back, or, esoterically as well as exoterically. Moses laid up the tables in the Ark and set up a guard of Levites 'dedicated to God'. The Levites did not finish their duties in less than twenty-five to fifty years, after which they went into reserve. Moses wanted his guard to consist of mature men; neither choirboys nor veterans. The stranger who approached the Tables was punished with death.

In what then did the Law that was so precious consist?

Patristic literature presents it as being composed of the ten commandments, the ritual and moral imperatives given out by Moses. This is playing with words. The commandments are the Law of Moses, not of the Eternal. And they are not secret — on the contrary. The Law is written, proclaimed and taught. It was a discipline and it was not hidden in the Ark.

The Tables of the Law are something extremely sacred, coming as they did from the hand of God; extremely precious, constituting a contract of power; extremely dangerous and no-one has access to them, not even the Levite guard, but the High Priest alone; and still it is to be reduced, by Solomon, to once a year. We are concerned then with a divine law.

It is written that the power promised to Israel derived from these Tables: then either they are a talisman or they are a *means* of power. But the Eternal is not a petty sorcerer who makes medals or amulets. It follows then that the Tables are a *means*.

They are the Tables of the Law, the Logos, the Word; of reason, measure, relationship, number.

'I have made everything with number, measure and weight,' says the Lord God in Genesis. The divine Law is the Law of Number, Measure and Weight. In the language of today we should call the Tables of the Law the Tables of the Cosmic Equation.

To possess the Tables, then, is to have the possibility of access to the great Law of unity that rules the worlds, of relating effects with their causes and consequently of *acting* on the phenomena that the causes produce as they diversify into plurality.

One sees that Moses was not deceiving the Hebrew people when, in the name of the Eternal, he promised them power and dominion *through* the Tables of the Law. But it goes without saying that he would only present the possibility of using this instrument of power to those who had made themselves worthy of it; and that is why he not only forbade access to the Tables but also took the greatest care to hide the light under a bushel.

Allowing that a man might succeed in breaking the triple defence of the armed Levites, the electrified Ark and the secret defences (those which gave the Philistines haemorrhoids), he would still be unable to make use of the

Tables unless he had been initiated into the secret of reading them. Moses gave such initiation in a commentary in Semitic language and in a writing that he perhaps devised; a cryptic writing in a numerical system that was later called the Cabbala. The secret then was well sealed up. More so even than it seems.

Since his commentaries, which constitute the sacred books, are in cypher, they must in no case be modified, even by an iota. Change would render the cryptography undecipherable. Thus, one begins to see why Etienne Harding, Saint Etienne, Abbot of Citeaux, although his Order was an Order of 'contemplatives', put the whole of his Abbey, after the conquest of Jerusalem, with such ardour to the study of the Hebraic texts, with the aid of learned rabbis from High Burgundy; and why Saint Bernard made a special journey across the Rhine to calm the anti-semitical fury of those who lived in that region who were, already, organising bloody pogroms.

It was because the Hebraic books constitute a 'treatise on the interpretation' of the Stone and the Jews are the depositories of it.

Perhaps we had better return to the Law. Whence came it? From God, who wrote it himself with his finger, on stone, readable in two ways. This is a miracle. But 'miracle' is a word men use for what passes their understanding; or for what it is wished they should believe. To involve God in a miracle is to subject him to the idea men make for themselves of the laws that govern the world. It is to confine him within *our* time and *our* space; to reduce him to the status of a demiurge, if not sorcerer.

All comes from God no doubt; but, at the human level, everything manifests according to man's interpretation.

Moses came from Egypt. Egyptian wisdom was centred in the Temple. Moses was a man of the Temple and was learned in all the wisdom of the Egyptians (Acts VII, 22). Although they did not make use of plastic materials, the diesel engine or detergents for washing up — all things that poison earth, air and water — the Egyptian ecclesiastical *élite* had knowledge that is written in the monuments, an alchemical science which has even retained the name of its field of activity, and a human science the greater part of whose aspects are still unknown to us. It is probable that Moses, on Sinai, inspired by God, reduced this science to formulas and since papyrus is fragile inscribed them on stone. The law is none the less divine for all that, like all true law.

A few more words about the Ark.

Knowledge, in no matter what kind, has only speculative interest. If it is to be of use to mankind, it must be translated into action. To bring a work into being there must be workers. Israel forgot this obvious principle, which is why it was never given to Israel itself to realise the work the detail of which is to be found in the Tables of the Law. Solomon, king of Jerusalem, had to appeal to Hiram, king of Tyre, to build his Temple.

The sons of Saint Benoit will not forget this.

Workmen are indispensable of course, but so is measure. Higher or lower, the pyramid of Cheops is only a fine heap of stones. Larger or smaller, the diapason only gives LA. One must have at disposal a valid measure, a common denominator between world and man. It would seem that as regards the Tables of the Law this was a unit of measurement which was laid in the Ark in the form of Aaron's Rod, the living baton. It vanished in Solomon's time.

No doubt Moses also laid in the Ark a unit of weight, the quantity of manna contained in a vessel. He said to Aaron, 'Take an urn and put in it an omer of manna and set the urn before the eternal that it may be kept from generation to generation.' An omer is the tenth part of an epha.

A question remains. Was the Ark still in the basement of Solomon's Temple at the time of the Crusades?

8 The Hidden Ark

It follows from the history of the Ark itself that it was in the subterranean parts of the Temple. The story is to be found in the historical parts of the Old Testament, from Moses until Solomon, after which it disappears from all but apocryphal writings.

Led by Moses, and strictly guarded, the Ark followed or preceded the people from the desert of Sinai to Horeb, through the country of Moab, the country of Gilead. After Moses died it crossed the Jordan under Joshua's leadership and entered Palestine, where it followed the vicissitudes of the fighting. It seems to have rested at Silo for some little time. In the days of Samuel the Philistines beat the Israelites and the Ark of God was captured and taken to Ashod, in the temple of Dagon, where it caused a good deal of havoc, notably when it struck the people of the town with haemorrhoids (it would be astonishing if the translation was correct: I lean to the interpretation that it was a matter of haemophilic casualties from which radio-activity was perhaps not lacking, possibly brought on by the manna).

From Ashod, always in the possession of the Philistines, the Ark was taken to Gath, then to Ekron, with the same effects on the people of those places. The Ark defends itself, which is not at all scientific in the current sense of the term; but one has to believe that it was furnished with some defensive spells.

Finally, scared, the Philistines returned it to the

Israelites, who took it to Kirjath-Jearim, whence David had it removed to Jerusalem, in his dwelling at Sion. Solomon must have had it placed in the Holy of Holies in the Temple he built.

After the Book of Joshua, there is scant mention of the Ark, except as a sacred object, a luck-bringer of whose profound importance writers were ignorant or pretended to be. David alone attached some importance to it otherwise than as an object of veneration. He danced before it, which we may ascribe to scorn for a fashionable snobbism.

It may well appear that David the musician, conqueror of material powers in the shape of Goliath, may have been a cabbalist and may have tried to acquire the knowledge written on the stone. He was in any case enough of a geomancer to fix the site of the future temple; a project which, having been a man of war, he was unable to realise but for which he assembled the materials.

This building had to be Solomon's work. Solomon was the man of peace, the Sage, the 'strong' man, initiate. We find in Kings I, iv. 29-31, 'And God gave Solomon wisdom and understanding exceeding much, and largeness of heart, even as the sand that is on the sea shore. And Solomon's wisdom excelled the wisdom of all the children of the east country, and all the wisdom of Egypt. For he was wiser than all men . . .'

This wise man built the Temple. Or, more exactly, he caused it to be built, for he had not a people of builders at his disposal, above all religious builders, initiates. He was obliged to address himself to Hiram, king of Tyre: 'I propose to build a house to the glory of the Eternal Name,' he wrote (*In nomini Dei da gloriam*, others will put it).

However, it was Solomon who gave the design; which assumes, among other skills, a knowledge of cosmic proportions and of standards of measurement. But Solomon was a Sage, learned, that is to say, in occult knowledge; he was therefore a cabbalist. He could read the holy Writings. He had the key to the decypherment of the Law. He possessed the Tables, Aaron's measuring-rod. He planned the Temple.

It would seem too that Solomon, the new Moses, had likewise written a new 'commentary' on the Tables of the Law; a commentary evidently in cypher which was at the same time his 'testament' as an adept: The Song of Songs. In this he made use of an ancient Egyptian theme, which was given out as of the highest initiatory importance; and if this love-song, apparently profane, was included among the sacred books, this was certainly not without reason. And it was not without reason that Saint Bernard devoted a hundred and twenty of his sermons to it.

Truly a fine subject of sacred literature for White Friars, this book crammed with erotic images whose first verse affirms and announces the hermetic theme:

'I am black but I am beautiful, daughters of Jerusalem.'

But alchemy and religious architecture seem inseparable.

When he refrained from introducing manual labour other than agriculture among his disciplines it may be that Moses wished to confine Israel to the simple function of guarding the Ark; but however this may be, thanks to Hiram-Abi the Phoenician, skilled in the use of the 'ancient measure', the Temple was built.

The initiatory tradition of 'manual magic' undoubtedly came to the Phoenicians from the builders of Egyptian temples. It was they, probably, who passed it on to the Greeks, through whom it reached the mediaeval West. The learned pundits and builders of churches assented willingly to the tradition of the 'sons of Abiram'. We shall come across them again.

As soon as the Temple was built Solomon caused the Ark to be placed in the Holy of Holies. The last direct

mention of it in the sacred books is found in Kings, I, viii.
12: 'Then spake Solomon, The Lord said that he would
dwell in the thick darkness. I have surely built thee an
house to dwell in, a settled place for thee to abide in for
ever.' After that there is no direct mention in the historical
books; only legends.

According to one of these, the son of Solomon and the
Queen of Sheba came to visit his father who, having
instructed him, gave the Ark into his care with fifty
Levites for this service. The Ark, at that time, had been
taken to Ethiopia, where it was still to be found.
According to another version, the son stole the Ark.

It is certain that the Christian clergy of Abyssinia claim
that they still hold the Ark, which the Patriarch alone is
allowed to set eyes on once a year, according to what was
laid down by Solomon for the High Priest.

It seems astonishing that Solomon should hand the Ark of
The Covenant over to his son, to take away, without protest
from the people, because it was clear proof that the
Eternal had chosen them and promised them dominion
over all other peoples. It would be equally astonishing if
Solomon's son was able to steal the Ark from the Holy of
Holies that was so amply guarded. Moreover, the Temple
was forbidden to strangers on pain of death. But it would
not seem at all impossible that Solomon should have had a
copy of the Tables made, or even of the Ark, to hand to
his son, no doubt after due instruction.

When Nebuchadnezzar took Jerusalem no mention of
the Ark was made among the articles of plunder. He had
the Temple burnt in 587 B.C. And the Ark burnt with it,
says Wegener.

But it is certain that the Ark was buried. Did not
Solomon say that it should dwell in darkness? This could
not be the case if it remained in the Holy of Holies.

There is still another proof of its interment.

It was the custom among the rabbis, after the disappearance of the Temple, to shut up food-offerings in a cupboard where they kept the rolls of the Torah. The offerings attracted mice and 'the rabbinical authority issued several decrees to put an end to this irregular interpretation of the texts; but what was to be done with the offerings that had been in contact with the sacred books? One could hardly throw them on the rubbish heap; they must end up in the ghénizah or cemetery for sacred objects. As to this, one recalls an ancient tradition: When the Ark of the Covenant was interred, the receptacle that contained the manna was borne to the ghénizah because it had been in contact with the Tables of the Law.'*

Well then, the Ark was buried. Even if this was not done by Solomon, it is certain that during the siege of Jerusalem it was the first thing to be hidden from possible conquerors. And if Nebuchadnezzar did not find it this must be because he did not dig deep enough, if that was what he sought after.

We come across mention of the Ark in the Document of Damascus, written Caraïte, dating from the first century of the Christian era. The Caraïtes seem near enough to the Essenes:

'But David had not read in the Book of the Law, sealed, that was in the Ark; and it was never opened, in Israel, after the death of Eliézer, of Joshua and of the Saviour. And as the ancients who sacrificed to Astarte became unclean, *it was hidden until* Caddoq rose up.'*

Flavius Josephus, in his Jewish Antiquities, mentions it as being at Ascalon.

I think it more likely that the Tables of the Law, made use of by Solomon at the proper times, were thereupon returned to the crypt, put to sleep like the princess awaiting the awakener, Prince Charming, at the time

* Del Medico: Manuscripts of the Dead Sea, according to Yom. 52b.

prescribed. For as it is said in the Song of Songs:

'Stir not up, nor awaken my love, until the hour She chooses!'

One cannot discard *a priori* the possibility that the Ark was discovered by the Arabs when they took Jerusalem. If mention of this had been made in Mohammedan writings it would most likely have been made in allegorical form. This could explain the veneration which Mohammedan legends profess for Suleiman ben Daoud, Solomon son of David, and the erection of the mosque El Aksa on the site of the Temple. It could also explain the stubbornness shewn by Jew and Mohammedan together in the defense of the Masjid-el-Aksa when the town was taken by the Crusaders. It could explain too the Mohammedan civilisation.

Were they not trying to gain the necessary time, by their desperate defence, to perfect the camouflage of the hiding-place where the Ark was buried?

Long before the Crusades a legend spread through the West concerning a mysterious priest John, almost immortal, who had founded a Christian Kingdom in some region towards the East and who owed both his success and his longevity to possession of the Ark of the Covenant. Throughout the Middle Ages men set out on a search for this mysterious kingdom whose exact geographical position no-one knew, some placing it in Persia, some in India, some even in China. Saint-Louis himself sent ambassadors who never came back.

Most likely the mysterious kingdom was Abyssinia, where legend placed the Ark stolen by Solomon's son; possibly the Copts of Egypt spread the rumour that it was really there, copy or original. And on all the evidence what interested the West in priest John's kingdom was the Ark, source of all power; for if monastic scholars had some enlightenment as to what the Ark was and what it contained it is likely that laymen, from kings to common men, thought of it as an extraordinary talisman, rich and powerful, forgetting what Saint Paul said of it: 'For the law having a shadow of good things to come, and not the very image of the things, can never . . .' (Hebrews, x. 1).

But scholar and common people alike were so convinced of its importance that one asks oneself whether the Crusades were not mounted with a view to getting hold of it.

9 The Return to France

Did the Templars find the Ark? One may think it would be impossible to give an absolutely certain answer to this; that there can be no absolute proof. The mission was secret and altogether secret has remained its outcome, defeat or success. There are nevertheless certain presumptions, and in such quantity that they may with good reason lead to at least a moral certainty.

First of all, we will mention, by way of reminder, the oral tradition that makes of the Knights Templar keepers of the Tables of the Law, through which they obtained power and initiation. With this we may connect the poem of Wolfram von d'Eschenbach, composed on a lost exploit of Gyot's, probably Guyot of Provins. This Wolfram von d'Eschenbach, who is said to have been a Templar — though there is no proof of this — for whom the Grail is a *stone*, makes the conqueror of the Grail a Grand Master of the Templars. And it would not seem that this knight wrote carelessly, or to compose a best seller. More conclusive is the return of the nine Knights in 1128, the story of which is told historically as follows:

In 1128 the king Baldwin II, victim of difficulties arising from the want of fighting men and free inhabitants in the Holy Land, sent the Pope a message asking for help. He asked Hugues de Payns to be his ambassador. Hugues de Payns was certainly a very remarkable man and noble enough in rank to play the part of ambassador which had to include, as well as Baldwin's message, an argumentation which the king judged him capable of sustaining. On the other hand, he was neither one of the king's counsellors, who were usually chosen for this kind of mission, nor did he hold any part of the Holy Land in fief. In fact, as we shall see, it was not the king who 'sent' Hugues de Payns; he took advantage of de Payns' departure to charge him with this mission.

And Hugues de Payns left with almost all, if not all, of his companions. According to a sure source at least five of them accompanied him and met at the Council of Troyes: Payen de Montdidier, Archambaud de Saint-Amand, Geoffroy Bisol, Rosal and Gondefroy. The guardianship of the pilgrims' routes certainly fell to second place.

It is clear that all or nearly all the knights were not sent off to carry a simple message. What's more, an order was received; Saint Bernard himself acknowledged in the most explicit manner, in the preliminaries to the rule he was about to give the Órder of the Temple, that he recalled the Knights and that their mission was fulfilled.

The introduction begins thus:

'Well has Damedieu (Dominus Deus or Notre-Dame?) wrought with us and our Saviour Jesus-Christ; who has set his friends of the Holy City of Jerusalem on march through France and Burgundy . . .'

'The work has been accomplished with *our* help. And the knights have been sent on the journey through France and Burgundy, that is to say Champagne, under the protection, as we shall see, of the Count of Champagne, where all precautions can be taken against all interference by public or ecclesiastical authority; where at this time one can best make sure of a secret, a watch, a hiding-place.'

And one is led to think that if so many of the knights took part in the expedition it is because they were escorting something that must be convoyed and guarded, something especially precious.

There are at the north door of Chartres, called the door

of the Initiates, two small columns, carved in relief, one
picturing the transport of the Ark by a couple of oxen,
with the inscription, *Archa cederis*; the other shewing an
Ark that a man is covering with a veil, or is taking hold of
with a veil, near a heap of corpses among which one
discerns a knight in his coat of mail, with the inscription,
Hic amititur Archa cederis (*amititur* probably for
amittitur). That subtle Latinist Eugéne Canseliet, writes to
me on this subject, 'The inscriptions are scarcely eloquent.
Archa cederis or "you are to work through the Ark"; *Hic
Amititur, archa cederis* or "Here things take their course;
you are to work through the Ark".'

Do we not see in them the explanation of certain
architectural features of the cathedral of Chartres the
interpretation of which is scientifically so far beyond what
can be allowed for in the knowledge of the epoch (and
probably even of our own) that only the use of a
document such as the Tables of the Law can throw light
on them? I shall come back to this point.

The scenes represented are evidently biblical. One
recognises the removal of the Ark and its loss after the
battle with the Philistines. However, without wishing to
make any perhaps too daring link-up with an eventual
removal of the Ark by the Templars, I must point out
something odd:

The Ark shewn in these carvings is a coffer furnished
with wheels, a coffer bound with iron bands, which oxen
are towing, contrary to what is said in II Samuel, vi. 3:
'And they set the ark of God upon a new cart . . . and . . .
they took it away.'

There can be no question of a stylisation of the
ensemble: the Ark-chariot, for in the scene of the
hecatomb or public sacrifice the man who is gripping the
Ark with a veil is gripping an Ark with wheels. Moreover, it
has been maintained — and this is not at all illogical — that
the four *kéroubim* were not Cherubim but wheels. The
wheel was relatively new in Moses' day. It still did nòt

exist at the time when the pyramids at Gizeh were built.

It is in any case astonishing that in representing the Ark the sculptor or image-maker as they called him in those days, who necessarily followed the instructions of the master-craftsman, should have shewn not the angel-Cherubim of which the Christian version of the scriptures speaks, but wheels affixed to the body of the Ark itself.

All the same, brought up on the scriptures, builders of cathedrals could hardly be ignorant that the Christian versions presume, for the carriage of the Ark on the arms of men, cross-bars inserted in rings (which must not be withdrawn) and not with axle-trees. Still, it is a man who lifts the veiled Ark with his naked arms.

Had the Master-Craftsman at Chartres (church of the companions and Templars if that is what it was) some special knowledge regarding this aspect of the Ark?

There are no other proofs of a removal of the Ark, or of a replica, into France. None except those that one does not look at because they are under your nose – the gothic cathedrals.

In 1128 Hugues de Payns came back to France. After that date, and during one hundred and fifty years more or less, comes what has been called the miracle of the gothic flowering.

More. The spread of the gothic style and of the Temple went together. In due course they will vanish together; not the gothic technique, of which Viollet-le-Duc knew well enough to create, sometimes, an illusion. 'Flamboyant' architecture of the XIVth century is something different; it is an ogival or pointed building with all the qualities you might ask for, except the principal. I will explain myself presently.

Another coincidence. The nine Knights were sent out by Bernard the Cistercian; gothic was born at Cîteaux. The whole gothic formula derives from the Cistercians and the 'Compagnons des Devoirs' – heirs of the builders of gothic cathedrals — make no mystery that they derive their characteristic 'feature', their descriptive geometry, indispensable for the erection of gothic monuments, from the Cistercian Order.

Another thing: if the romanesque only comes to its fullness, from the day of the Roman and Byzantine, after many 'improvements', the gothic appears at one blow, complete, whole, and throughout the West. 'One can hardly believe,' writes Régine Pernoud, 'that such a development, at the same time so vigorous and so swift, can have been due to a new decorative formula.' But we are dealing, not with a formula of this kind, but with an initiatory means of civilisation. Someone awakened the Sleeping Beauty, and all her train were awakened at the same time. And they worked with new processes on a new cultural basis, commercially and artistically.

There is more in the gothic than a series of technical solutions. There is a building of temples that are gates to the Kingdom of God; and this requires a higher science than that of the calculation of forces and resistances. It demands knowledge of the laws of numbers, matter, spirit and if it is to work in the souls of men, knowledge of the laws of physiology and psychology. Someone revealed all this.

If it is not the Ark, if it is not the Tables of the Law, the knights Templar must have brought back an extraordinary initiatory document to the West.

10 The Mystery of the Towers

The dolmen of Chartres and its covered passage were hidden underground. So were most dolmens. Those we see in the open air owe this to the rains that at length washed away the surrounding earth. It is likely that most tumuli or mounds hide a dolmen in their flanks.

The Roman legions established, without any doubt, on the Mound of Chartres a camp or small fort of which a basement wall remains, on the eastern side of the cathedral, under the junction of the apse with the choir. This wall did not encroach on the Mound itself and was possibly built on an earlier and enclosing wall, a cyclopean wall like that which is still to be seen, or parts of it, at Saint-Odile — another holy place — in Alsace.

And now we must consult the historians who have examined monuments earlier than the cathedral itself. They are all agreed that there was once a gallo-roman temple to which an edifice of the earliest Christian times succeeded, having the same orientation as the cathedral and whose rounded apse made use of the underparts of a gallo-roman defensive tower, as at Bourges. This, which formed a crypt, is still extant and is known as 'the cavern of Saint-Lubin'. In the IXth century this cavern was part of a church called the 'Church of Gislebert'. Some massive walls of this are extant in the foundations, and thanks to this we know that this church too had the same orientation; and that it did not encroach on the sacred Mound. It was wholly destroyed by fire on the night of 7-8th September, 1020.

1020. This was a notable epoch in romanesque architecture; the epoch during which Christianity decked itself with 'a display of white churches'; for this was the time when after a labour lasting five centuries the Benedictine abbeys succeeded in constituting a corps, a lay brotherhood of builders, affiliated to the Order, to which they could appeal for protection if necessary.

After the abbeys, where they trained their workmen, the Benedictines were able to put lay builders at the disposal of the secular church, often under the direction of monastic master-craftsmen, such as the Abbé of Saint-Bénigne-de-Dijon, Guillaume de Volpiano, who came to build and teach in Normandy.

The church of Gislebert having been destroyed, the bishop of Chartres, Fulbert, immediately undertook its rebuilding, asking Bérenger, described as *artifex bonus*, good architect, to take charge of the work.

It was Fulbert, or this same Bérenger (we know little about them) who restored, if this had not been done before, the covered way, in the form of two galleries, half underground, that led to the dolmenic chamber of the Black Virgin, the Virgin who is to give birth to a Child, Our-Lady-of-Under-the-Earth. Like his predecessor, Fulbert respected the Mound: the two galleries encompassed without encroaching on it at any point. They came together in a semicircle around the cavern of Saint-Lubin; the rectangular dolmenic well opened in the north gallery.

These two galleries and Fulbert's round-point still exist beneath the aisles and choir of the present church called, wrongly, the crypt; a more exact designation would be 'the lower church'.

There is a tradition that the builders' guilds, at least the 'Children of Solomon', held ceremonies of initiation in this crypt.

Fulbert's upper church followed the ground-plan of the lower church under the aisles. The nave, whose width was that of the present nave, stood on the Mound. It had a sort of transept where the second bay of the choir is now — mystical and anatomical centre of the cathedral, between the stained glass window of Notre-Dame-de-la-Belle-Verrière and the chapel of the Virgin of the Pillar.

Fulbert's church was romanesque in style and covered in wood, smooth and without abutment to give lateral support. It had a flat facade and its belfries rose, one to the north, near the apse, the other at the extremity of the southern aisle.

M. René Merlet, historian of the cathedral, who had already found and uncovered the dolmenic well, was also to find an iconographical document which he published and which enables us to form some idea of what Fulbert's church was like.

Marvellous things are told of it.

In September 1134 a fire ravaged the town of Chartres. It burnt down the Hospital which stood near the church and reached the church itself. In this disaster the church lost its western porch and the adjoining belfry. It was in consequence of this fire that the building of the towers we know today was put in hand, not near the church but well in front of it. With the object, so the historians say, of making Fulbert's church longer.

Tradition replied, is that so?

When history and tradition are not in agreement, it is safe to bet, almost as a certainty, that it is the historians, makers of history, who are deceived. And tradition speaks with the pen of Monseigneur Devoucous, who was bishop of Autun during the last century.

A temple, Christian or other, is not built like a hangar. Apart from a site indicated by its 'divine' qualities, it was requisite to begin with that some 'inspired' man should communicate its dedication (that is to say, the formula) in sacred language, the letters of which, cabalistically read, will disclose numbers. by which — and their relations — the sacred precinct should be determined in its length and breadth.

Through the relations between the astronomical heavens and the site, on a given date, some particularly learned man deduced the unit of measurement — today we should call it the module — to be employed. Measure, orientation and the numbers were then communicated to the master-craftsman, (but never it seems the dedication) who, on the basis of these preliminary data, would choose his stone — some English churches are built in stone from Caen — and, in the style of the period, adapted to the men of the time and place, and in accordance with the rhythm of the material chosen, determine the harmonic proportions of the future monument. This established, with the aid of a few sketches, the master-craftsman laid out, within the enclosure determined by the dedication, the plan itself, *on the ground*, with the measure and line that is at the same time rule, set-square and compass on a grand scale.

There are no such ground-plans in existence, only sketches. The plan results from some cerebral event which the architect cuts out on the ground. The master-craftsman was governed by the quality of the site, to which he adapted his performance: one did not attain mastership without an initiation and that was not merely a professional formality. The unity of the monument, the influence it was to exert over men, came, in the deepest sense, from the dedication.

It follows that to change the proportions, and the dimensions, of a Temple was equivalent to its destruction, making it useless. You cannot add a column to the Parthenon without destroying it. If you double the dimensions you get, not a double Parthenon, but that atrocity which is the Madeleine.

It follows from this that the towers were built for another church than Fulbert's; a new church based on a new dedication; a church that foresaw perhaps a new use for Fulbert's, which was not perhaps, in style, the existing church, but it certainly had the same dimensions and proportions. It was probably for this that the 'royal entrance', from which the master-craftsman did not wish to part company, was constructed; for this too that the stained-glass window of Notre-Dame-de-la-Belle-Verrière and the three great western bays were destined.

One might mention the case of Cluny, which was 'lengthened' but the Abbey itself was not involved. A narthex was added which is not comprised in the sacred part of the edifice.

Historians have more or less agreed that this is exactly what it was wished to do at Chartres: to build a narthex in front of the edifice. This was admissible; but the geometrical conditions that constitute the plan of Chartres, all of which proceed from the sacred centre in the choir, shew that its harmonic development comes to a head in the towers and that these are therefore the true *entrance* to the cathedral and that the narthex, had there been one, would not have exceeded their breadth (the proof of this will be given further on).

And one must hold, for it is logical, that the geometrical determinants, which are the basis of the existing church, were already laid down when the building of the towers began.

One is astonished to notice that the position of the towers corresponds *exactly* with the development of the three traditional tables in the church as it stands and *exactly* with the position of the buttresses necessary to the support of the *existing* gothic vault.

Finally, the height of the south belfry, which was finished well before the building of the nave was begun, connects harmoniously with the dimensions of the existing cathedral. One can hardly avoid the impression that the monument was in view not long after 1134 and that its dedication must have been communicated about then — even before Fulbert's church disappeared — and that the two towers, exterior to the main fabric, were built for the future cathedral of which they were to constitute the most solid support.

Forty years later, the master-craftsman had only to give living form — but with what art and science! — in the style of his time to the preliminary data, as he did for the *necessary* western rose over the great stained-glass window.

But in 1194, it was all burnt down except the towers.

11 In 26 Years . . .

Let us repeat the history of it.

The church went up in flames on Friday, 11th June, 1194. 'The intensity of the fire was such that woodwork and roof were utterly destroyed and nearly all the walls fell in. As soon as it was possible to estimate the consequences of this disaster, it was seen that only the IXth and XIth century crypts had been saved from all damage thanks to the solidity and thickness of the vaults; the two XIIth century belfries likewise withstood the flames.'* Neither were the great western windows damaged, nor the window of Notre-Dame-de-la-Belle Verrière: it may be they had been taken down for the time being, for some other reason.

And although, according to René Merlet, the lower parts of the XIth century ·chevet, or apse with radiating chapels, could only with difficulty be utilised by way of foundation for the new round-point, the new cathedral, *immediately put in hand*, was built *in its entirety*, except the porticos, that is to say the exterior decoration, between 1194 and 1220. Twenty-six years!

Let us meditate on all the aspects of this problem, resolved so happily: ground-plan, material, labour-force, execution, finance.

The ground-plan first of all.

Independently of the time necessary for its conception — which could be the result of illumination, it is

* René Merlet: 'La Cathédrale de Chartres.'

true — the erection of arches with the reach of those at
Chartres, the widest gothic vault known and one of the
highest, sets an extremely difficult problem as regards the
locking together of the forces of lateral expansion — fundamental key to solidity. Apart from the two western towers,
so exactly and so thoughtfully placed beforehand, this locking together necessitated six more, two at each end of the
transepts and two at the intersection of the rounded apse
with the sides of the choir; towers whose weight at least,
resistance to thrust and their outlines must be calculated.
Next it was necessary to calculate the weight, outline and
distance apart of the flying and other buttresses which must
take the expanding lateral forces of the high vault and the
lower vaults of the aisles. And all this within the space
measured out by the dedication. How much time would an
architect, an architect's office, ask for the carrying out of
such a project? Yet by the end of 1194 the work was in hand.

This would seem to imply that the master-craftsman was
on the spot, ready; that he knew already what he was
about; that his plan was prepared, at least in his head; that
he had chosen the quarry for his material, had his
labour-force picked. And that he himself, with strange
celerity, had been appointed, forewarned, summoned.

And as far as I know, nobody has pointed out, at
Chartres, any single thing to be corrected.

The problem of material was easy to solve. The quarries
at Berchères-les-Pierres were already known and exploited.
It was these that furnished the fabric of the towers. As
regards transport to the Mound, we know that this
problem was overcome with the benevolent help of
pilgrims. And there was no seigneur so great that he did
not think it an honour to put on harness and help draw the
wagons. Although, naturally, oxen and horses could give
better service, and La Beauce was rich in draught-animals.

But how do we explain that the labour-force was so
easily found and so soon put to work?

One does not have to be a member of the craft to realise that the building of the cathedral at Chartres was not the work of apprentices and that all concerned, carpenters, stone-cutters and masons, were masters in their art. However, between 1194 and 1220 churches and cathedrals were being built throughout France; churches and cathedrals that were not the work of apprentices. In Normandy alone, not far away, there were built, in the XIIth century, fifteen great churches, of which eight were abbeys; in the XIIIth, thirteen, of which five were abbeys. For the whole of France we must reckon that between 1150 and 1250 one hundred and fifty monuments were put in hand, among them churches of the dimensions of those in Paris, Reims, Amiens, Sens, Rouen.

How was it possible to assemble qualified labour so swiftly?

And what is to be said about finance?

Except Chartres (apart from the towers) no cathedral in France was built in one sweep. The building of nearly all French churches was interrupted at one time or another for want of money to pay the workmen. Nothing of the kind happened during the building of Chartres.

Chartres, a small town of some few thousands of inhabitants, brought off what was beyond prosperous cities like Paris, Amiens, Rouen. But was it really Chartres that provided the finance? And what can have been the importance of this building that such means were set going?

Was Chartres the 'Golden Book' of the West in which Sages wrote the message of their wisdom? Anyone who tries to spell out this book written in stone will come across strange coincidences.

To begin with, we have a situation which is the gift of Earth. Then come three men. The first is inspired by God.

He communicates the dedication, which is in sacred language, cabalistic, like a reflection of the Word in this place.

The second is a man of learning. He translated into Numbers, which are relationships, the letters and words of the dedication. He gave the Number of the place, which is the relationship between place and world and the unit of measurement.

Third is the master-craftsman. For him Numbers become verticals and curves expressed in matter, shapes and proportions in stone, weights and the thrust of ogives.

To the wise men we ascribe the Word; to the learned, the Number; to the workmen, harmony realised in matter. To someone unknown, analysis, hypothesis, the play of spirit . . . we ask questions.

We can no longer interrogate the master-craftsman, no doubt; but he has left some answers, written in a harmony of stone. It is enough to ask the right questions. The cathedral answers them.

12 Line and Measure

The Cathedral says, 'All the answers are written here.' All that should be said is said. What has vanished is only the work of those barbarous children, men, whether bishop or lamplighter, despot or leader of revolutions. 'In the name of religion they have shattered its religious symbols. In the name of liberty they have broken down the doors of liberty. In the name of light they have shattered the doors of light. But not all the answers have vanished. Interrogate.'

I looked for the centre, the point of departure.

The greatest oak springs from a point in an acorn, the germ without which there is no oak, great or small.

The 'germ' of Chartres was carefully indicated. Three times. It is the telluric concentration-point of the site; or, to speak like our ancestors, 'The Head of the *Wouivre*'; the head on which the divine Mother places her heel. This centre has always been known and of the three indications placed by the master-craftsman two remain. The one that has gone is the stone of the high altar. Until the XVIth century it stood very near this point, between the second and third bays of the choir and the officiating priest, returning from the altar, always stood there.

In Fulbert's romanesque church this was the crossing of the false transepts.

In the XVIth century need was felt to remove the altar to the bottom of the sanctuary; but the choir-stalls were already right over this spot. It was surmounted at that time by a spire in carved wood, higher than the spire at the crossing of the transepts, in which were some little bells of the kind known as 'babblers'. The spire disappeared in the fire of 1836 which made havoc of the roof without however doing any damage to the vault. The beams of the 'Forest' (name by which the combination of beams which form the roofs of cathedrals is known) were replaced by metal girders. This was undoubtedly a grave mistake and an injury to the monument's magnetic power. Recently the altar has again been moved to the crossing of the transepts; that is to say, in front of the area where the old rood-screen shut off the mystical part of the church. Ignorance is always with us.

The centre, where the altar *ought* to stand, is in the middle of the second bay of the choir. This bay is still indicated, to the south-east, by the window of Notre-Dame-de-la-Belle-Verrière and to the north-west by the chapel of Notre-Dame-du-Pilier. Besides, this bay, centre and origin of the whole, is framed, in the aisles, between the first and second collateral, by round pillars, bare, without colonnettes; two on one side, two on the other, the only ones of this kind in the aisles. It is easily seen that the necessary pointers are not wanting.

It is round this centre that a cathedral was built.

How? Let tradition answer first.

Traditionally, the first sign that a temple is under construction is the 'pillar' erected at the sacred centre. This, soon to disappear, symbolised a relation between Earth and Heaven. The real. The reality of stars and sun.

We must not confuse the Temple-Pillar with the pillars over which there is some question in the Temple of Solomon. The Temple-Pillar under reference is the first sign that a temple is issuing from the earth; the first relationship between the site and the sky that turns about it.

The building of a temple, Christian or other, remains in many respects mysterious. The height of the basic pillar had capital importance in the sense that through the play of solar shadows it indicated the dimensions whose relationships were a projection of those obtaining between celestial bodies; which is the law of the rhythms that govern life.

The four seasons played a preponderant rôle, which put three limits to the shadow thrown at the time of the two solstices and the two equinoxes. Triple enclosure within the life of Earth unfolds in a given place.

The pillar served likewise for the planetary and zodiacal sights that gave it position, not only on Earth but in relation to the planets and fixed stars.

Moses, who by means of the Tables of the Law in reality gave the pillar of the Temple, is represented on the north porch at Chartres holding in his arms a pillar which is a temple-pillar, a pillar with capital. And the Wouivre is climbing it in the shape of a little winged dragon.

Theoretically, it is the shadow of this pillar that will mark the first enclosure of the holy place, within which a ritual will evolve. And this enclosure is the first table. Its proportions are fixed by a tradition, which is a form of knowledge, together with the dimensions which the shadow of the pillar will mark.

It is evidently necessary that I should explain myself.

In the year 1964 the Society for the study of traditional Sciences, The Friends of Atlantis, lit the Fire of Saint John on a property in the suburbs of Paris. A delegation from the *Compagnons des Devoirs du Tour de France* came to carry the flame in ritual procession. They wore colours and carried beribboned sticks.

Before the chanting and the perambulation, hands clasped, in ritual manner around the flames, one of them spoke. He spoke — why not give the name — about Raoul

Vergez, companion-carpenter of the Duties, called Béarnais-l'Ami du-Tour-de-France, author of those two remarkable books on the companionship, *Les Tours Inachevées* and *La Pendule à Solomon.** As a carpenter, he was also creator of most of the church spires rebuilt in Normandy and Brittany after the ravages of the battle of 1944. He spoke and, I forget in what connexion, quoted the traditional enigma:

Three tables bore the Grail, a round one, a square one and a rectangular. All three have the same surface and their Number is 21. The rectangular table is that of the Eucharist. The mystical table, Christian, that which supports the altar and, indeed, the choirs of Christian churches are as a rule rectangular.

There have been other rectangular tables, as in Egyptian and Greek temples; square ones as in Gallo-Roman tables and in Saint Sophia at Constantinople, or again the Holy of Holies in the Temple of Solomon; round tables, as in the round churches of the Templars. But the choir at Chartres is rectangular.

There without doubt was the way in to the mystery of the cathedral's construction. But it was still necessary to solve the riddle of the Number 21. The answer is simple in fact. We are to read, not 21 but 2 and 1.

We are confronted then with a rectangular table whose length is twice its width.

I knew I was on the right road. First, because the ratio 2 to 1 is exactly that of the Egyptian and Greek temples; likewise of Solomon's Temple as far as the Holy of Holies. Next because this figure enjoys some geometrical properties that are rather interesting. A rectangle with the ratio 2 to 1 has a diagonal equal to $\sqrt{5}$. If we add to this diagonal the width of the rectangle and divide the new length by 2 we obtain a length equal to $(\sqrt{5} + 1)/2 = 1.618$, which is the Golden Number, limit of Fibonacci's series.

* Julliard, ed.

Apart from various properties which the Number possesses — which is a relationship with unity — and about which some extremely learned works have been written — it possesses the following:

$$\frac{1.618}{0.618} = (1 + 1.618) = (1.618 \times 1.618) = 2.618.$$

Now, 2.618 x 12/10 = 3.1416 = Pi. 3.1416, the constant that allows us to find the perimeter and surface of a circle the diameter of which is known. And 12/10 is the interval of a third in music; the interval between the major and minor scale.

We shall come across this interval with regard to the elevation of the cathedral; but the important thing is that the rectangular 2/1 Table contains the root of trans-formation of an angular into a circular surface; from which arises the possibility of deducing the surface of the round Table from that of the rectangular. It is a question then of squaring the circle; not at all on the basis of laboratory mathematics but that of the geometry of building.

One ought to be able to find such circle-squaring somewhere or other. If this holy place of the Gauls is indeed what I am little by little persuading myself, the three tables with the same surface should be written into it.

I set myself to measuring the cathedral.

Unhappily, whereas one may be conscious of harmony it does not lend itself easily to analysis. And, without at least turning away visitor, beadle and cleric, it is scarcely possible to use measuring chains in the cathedral or to instal the surveyor's apparatus.

I had to have recourse to drawing and diagram. Various difficulties ensued, which, besides, led me to certain unexpected reflections.

The cathedral seems to have grown like something in nature, a plant, a tree. A tree is round certainly, but if one takes a section of it this is no longer the case, any more than the two sides of a face are symmetrical.

The geometry of nature is only true in the main. In detail, a natural geometrical form is never exact, in the sense in which the mathematical don understands it. The pentagon of a flower with five petals is not regular. If it were, I fancy the flower would not look 'real'. Its irregularity is its personality, which does not come through the drawing one may make of it.

All the same, if the cathedral of Chartres is perfectly 'regular' for the tourist this is not so in a drawing or plan, except in its general effect when certain anomalies are removed.

There *are* certain anomalies, which do not seem to have been intended, and it is easily understood that the system of measurement employed by the builders may not have had an absolutely scientific precision. Human measurements, depending on eye and hand, are never anything but approximations, above all on this scale.

But there are other 'defects', and these are quite clearly intended. They are also imperceptible to the eye, as if the plant-cathedral had shot up, under the hand of a master craftsman, in accord with a law, that to him was authoritative, with life of its own.

Yet this cannot happen independently of the master-craftsman's will, for no technical fault, which would have exposed itself through subsidence or collapse, is to be found. Is this the outcome of a private mathematic of which we no longer have the data? Then what knowledge, what elevation of thought, had these anonymous men? Or indeed what natural affinity with all nature?

As to these irregularities, intended or not, it follows, as regards the metrical solutions I am about to put forward, that I have had to confine myself to approximation. For example, with reference to the width of the choir from axis of pillar to axis of pillar, I have chosen the mean of different measurements by different authorities,

16.40 metres, which assumes in practice a measure of 0.82 metres for the builder.

It goes without saying that if this figure is wrong by some millimetres there will be slight errors of measurement, but not, I believe, proportional.

Because of ignorance I made use of arithmetical calculation for the work of analysis. It is a means. But it goes without saying that the master of Chartres made no calculations. He was too knowledgeable. A measure, a line, were enough for him.

But the measure does not matter whatever it is. It is written in the proportions of Earth and, perhaps, of Heaven. A line is not used haphazard; it serves to draw out the ruling forms, which are a projection of the music of the spheres; a projection in rhythms which unfold in the image of the Great Law.

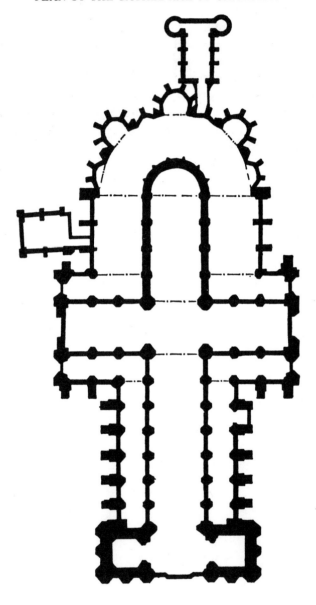

13 The Mystery of the Plan

Our point of departure is the Mound, and on the Mound the sacred Centre where the pillar of the Temple was set up.

The Mound, which must be enclosed but never encroached on, has a width already determined by Fulbert's church. The rectangular table then must have a length double this width. It is enough, when we are trying to settle it, to place one of the angles, the central axis being known.

This angle will be established by the shadow of the pillar, at sunrise at the equinox, cutting the north-east flank of the Mound.

There is a good deal of imprecision about this procedure. The shadow is fugitive and it is not so easy to fix a shadow cast by the rising sun. But an identical result may be obtained by means of azimuthal markings, of which there certainly is one to the east of the cathedral, on the 'butte d'Archevilliers', where in other days there should have been a dolmen. A sight can also be taken on the pole-star. Other procedures were possible: they do not matter much. What does matter is that, given the inclination of the cathedral to the parallel, the western angle of the table is found to be exactly that which the shadow of the pillar would mark out at sunrise at the equinox.

The rectangular table, then, is easily constructed by taking from this angle twice the length of the width of the

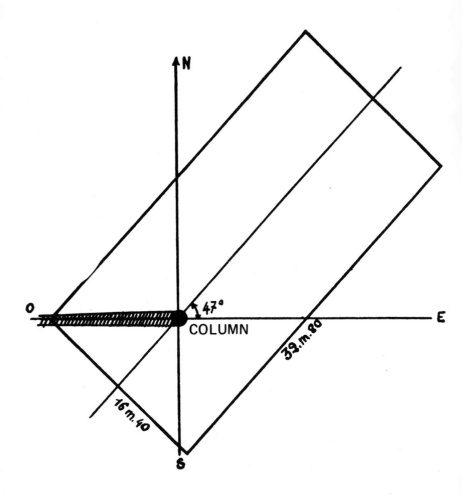

The width of the table is determined by the width of the 'sacred mound' to be enclosed. Traditionally, it is for the Sun to 'mark' the boundaries: for a given height of the pillar, the shadows thrown will be in harmonic relations with cosmic times and distances.

The measurements of the cathedral prove that the position of the base of the table with reference to the pillar is exact, not for an angle of $47°$ but for an angle of $46° 54'$. This is the actual inclination of the cathedral to the parallel.

Mound, say 32.80 m. The base of the table will be 7.68 m from the Centre.

The width of the table is 20 measures of 0.82 m (the Temple of Solomon had a width of 20 measures). Its length is 40 measures and its surface 800 measures squared, say, 537.92 m^2.

It should be mentioned that the base of the table does not correspond with the base of the existing choir, which ends at the great pillars at the crossing of the transepts, but with the ancient base which was marked by the rood-screen that was destroyed during the XVIIIth century.

The construction of a square table having the same surface presents no difficulty since it is enough to take the main axis of the rectangular table as its diagonal. This gives at once the width of the second enclosure and marks the limit of the first aisles of the choir, which is also that of the aisles of the nave, from the base of one wall to the base of the wall opposite.

The square has obviously the same surface as the rectangular table. Its side is 28 measures 284, say, 23.192 m.

But here we come on something extraordinary. The figure, 23.192 m, is strangely close to one tenth the side of the base of the Pyramid of Cheops, which one estimates, according to the authors already quoted, at between 230.30 and 232.80 m. The surface of the pyramidal base is therefore one hundred times that of the Tables of Chartres.

Not less extraordinary is the fact that the angle of inclination of this Pyramid — about 51° 25′ (the angle can no longer be measured exactly because the polished limestone facing has disappeared) — should be the angle on which the figure that gives the cathedral all its meaning and rhythm is constructed. It is the shape of a heptagonal star, commonly known as the star with seven points.

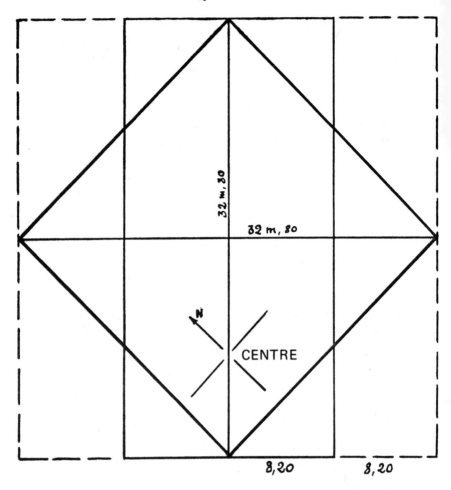

32 m, 80

32 m, 80

CENTRE

8,20   8,20

The reconstruction of the square Table on the main axis of the rectangular Table is soon done. The perpendicular diagonal gives the width of the first aisles of the choir and of the nave. The surface of the square Table, equal to that of the rectangular Table, is 537.92 metres; and the side of the square Table, $\sqrt{537.92} = 23.193$ m.

The side of the Pyramid of Cheops is given by different authors thus: Jomard, 230.902 m. Flinders Petrie, 230.364 m. Moreux, 232.805 m. One can only use approximations: it is difficult to measure exactly a pyramid whose facing has disappeared.

It is well to recall that the septenary symbolises incarnation, the descent of the Holy Three into the material quaternary. It is the Number of Earth vivified by the divine current; and this in geometrical form is the symbol of the Black Virgin.

The seven-pointed star is easily seen in the plan of the cathedral. It is enough to prolong the base-line of the rectangular table. The meeting of this line with the outer faces of the walls of the transeptal porches — the porches not included — gives two points of the star whose centre is the sacred centre itself.

As one of the branches of the star is identical with the axis of the cathedral, it is easy to discern the other branches.

But for the craftsman it was not the same thing. For him, the work went the other way round; it began, that is to say, with the construction of the star. It is from this that he will obtain his round-point, the width of the second aisles of the choir, the length and breadth of the transepts, the length of the cathedral and its area (emprise). Finally, it is this that will enable him to construct the round table with the same surface as the other two. And no doubt much else that the analyst has not known how to see.

The cathedral replies. And not with figures, which shews well enough that at no time did the master-craftsman have to make the smallest calculation; not, doubtless, that he would not have been capable of it, but because calculation, intellectual and quantitative, might have led to in-harmonious departures. Line and measure were enough for everything.

It follows moreover that a simple drawing of shapes or geometrical figures could perfectly well take the place of verbal interpretation. The metrical solutions that I am going to give are only put in so that the reader may follow the evolution of such shapes or figures in the dimensions of the church.

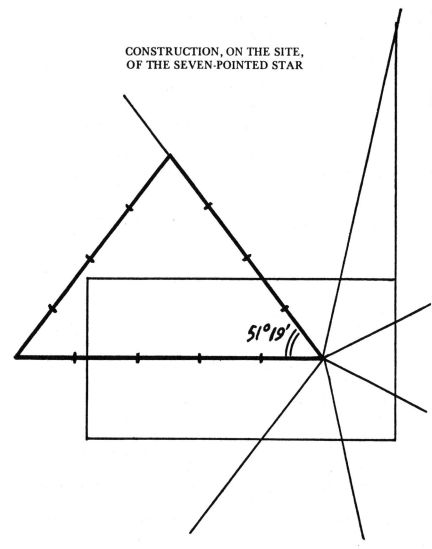

CONSTRUCTION, ON THE SITE,
OF THE SEVEN-POINTED STAR

51°19'

The so-called Druid's cord with twelve knots and thirteen equal segments allows of the construction, on the site, of different shapes. Thus for instance the right angle, by the use of twelve segments forming the triangle of Pythagoras; likewise, by arranging the segments in the ratio 5, 4, 4, an isosceles triangle with two angles of 51° 19', very near the seventh part of a circle (51° 25' 42" 8/10).

It will be noticed that an isosceles triangle outlines a pyramid, full face.

Ah! the Academics (dons) will say, but does not this man know that just like the squaring of the circle the division of a circle into seven equal arcs is impossible geometrically?

Possibly the Academics are right. At least they have not yet found the answer to these problems with the drawing-pen. But we, here, are on another plane, that of the cathedral of Chartres, or even, if you like, on the plane of building in general, where, even if the problems are solved the actual building would be subject to human and instrumental error.

In addition, the master craftsman does not 'calculate', in the sense in which the word is understood scholastically; the master-craftsman builds on the spot. He has no desire to compose a plan, but only to make his cathedral a living entity with a life of its own. He works, not in the abstract or ideal, but in the matter he is to animate; and to do this he makes use of rhythmical proportions which correspond with a living, vegetable, mathematic.

In fact, on the ground, the division of a circle into seven parts is perfectly feasible to a sufficient approximation, above all when the dimensions are great enough to allow of a certain amount of experiment, and that with measure and line alone.

The cord with twelve knots, which makes thirteen segments, of the Druids was amply sufficient since, if it is arranged in the form of an isosceles triangle with sides in the ratio 5, 4 and 4, you have two angles of 51° 19', while arithmetic gives, for the seventh part of 360°, 51° 25' 42" 86/100, an error of about 6' 42".

On large surfaces correction is easy by making the partition in the contrary direction and interpolating the error. Thus, one may consider the drawing of this partition perfectly feasible with an exactitude more than sufficient on the ground-plan of the building.

And then . . . it is not altogether to be excluded that the master craftsman at Chartres may have had a much better

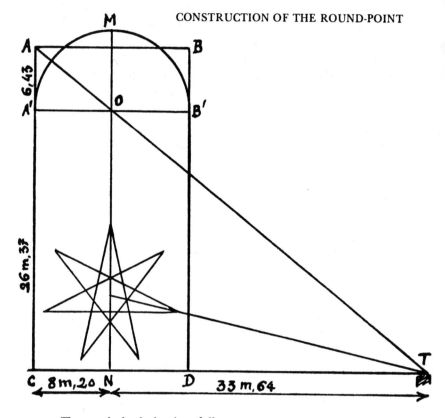

The metrical solution is as follows:

Suppose a table ABCD; MN is its main axis, and T the point of the star that marks the transept. The line AT cuts the axis at O and determines two similar triangles, ACT and ONT. Thus, AC/CT = ON/NT, whence (AC x NT)/CT = ON. Replacing the lengths by their numerical values, we get:

$$\frac{32.80 \times 33.64}{41.84} = 26.371. \text{ Whence,}$$

OM = CN = 8.20
NM = 8.20 + 26.37 = 34.57

The rectangle A′ ABB′ = 6.43 x 16.40 = 105.452; therefore, the semi-circle with centre O and radius OA′ (8,20) has for surface:

$$\frac{8.20^2 \times 3.1416}{2} = 105.620$$

procedure at his disposal. The procedure used in building a pyramid perhaps.

Let us then draw a seven-pointed star around the Centre, the highest point being the axis of the monument. Two of the lateral points, we observe, cut prolongations of the base of the rectangular table exactly at points on the outer limit of the transepts, thus determining their length.

· Traditionally – but it is impossible to confirm this – this dimension would be given in the assignment of numbers contained in the dedication.

However it may be, these two points, one of them at least, are particularly important, because they will allow of the drawing of the apse (round-point of the choir) and the round table with the same surface as the rectangular.

In effect, the master-craftsman is at grips with a leading difficulty, that of the round-point. As a result of the existence of the lower church – and foreseeing an ambulatory – he had to finish off his rectangular table with a semicircle without changing the surface area.

However, if you join the point of the star which marks the transept at the higher angle opposite the table, the point where this line cuts the axis of the table is the centre of a semi-circle with the width of the table for diameter and a surface-area practically the same as that of the rectangle it replaces.

The development of the rectangular table into a round-point is clearly an adaptation of gothic to romanesque; the basic Gothic plan being, it would seem, a straight rather than a rounded apse as at Notre-Dame de Laon.

The same point in the transept will be used in the construction of the round table. To make such a table with the same surface-area as a square or rectangular table involves squaring the circle, a geometrical impossibility that has been fully demonstrated. The integral calculus

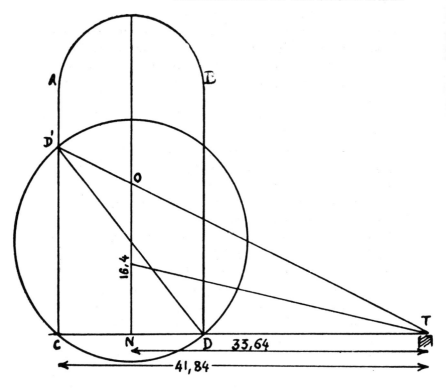

'The metrical solution is as follows:
O being the mid-point of the great axis of the rectangular table, the line TO cuts the line AC at D′, forming two similar triangles: D′CT and ONT. Therefore D′C/CT=ON/NT; whence, D′C=(ON x CT)/NT. Substituting values for lengths:

$$D′C = \frac{16.40 \times 41.84}{33.64} = 20.396$$

Besides, we have $D′D^2 = D′C^2 + CD^2$. $D′D^2 = (20.396)^2 + (16.40)^2 = 684.95$ and $D′D = \sqrt{684.956} = 26.172$.
The circle having D′D for diameter has for surface:

$$(684.956/4) \times 3.1416 = 537.96 \text{ m}^2$$

Thus, the surface of the rectangular table being 537.92^2, there is a difference of only 4 centimetres^2.
The radius of the round table thus constructed is 13.086 m, whereas, it should have been 13.085 metres, an error of 1 millimetre or, if preferred, 1/13,000.

itself can only give an approximation to the constant Pi. This is true, at least, for laboratory mathematics; in practice, one may obtain, geometrically speaking, an approximation quite sufficient to ensure that there is no false agreement.

It might seem astonishing that the 'squaring of the circle', which has become proverbial as an allegory of the impossible, should have so disquieted our ancestors, who clung to the hope of a geometrical solution.

I think we must see in it the search for a 'gate', a key to the passage from one world to another; a secret of initiation in some sense. The search has always been spiritual rather than directly material, very close and sufficient answers having been known in distant antiquity.

The meaning of the phrase 'to square the circle' was not the same for philosophers as for surveyors; as is the case with the meaning of the phrase 'the marriage of fire and water' for alchemists, who are not in the least concerned with steam engines.

However this may be, so much importance has been attached to the problem of a geometrical solution, that one is bound to suppose there is some secret hidden in it . . . a secret and key to a vital enigma.

If at the point of the star that marks the limit of the transept, and which has already been utilised for the construction of the rounded apse, one draws a line joining the middle of the rectangular table and one prolongs it to the opposite side of the table, it cuts the side at a certain point. If one connects this point with the opposite and lower angle, the distance between these two points has a value very close to the diameter of a circle with the same surface-area as the rectangular and square tables.

The construction of the round Table is not, it is clear, an unrestricted enterprise. It is this Table, above all else, that decides the placing of the great pillars at the base of

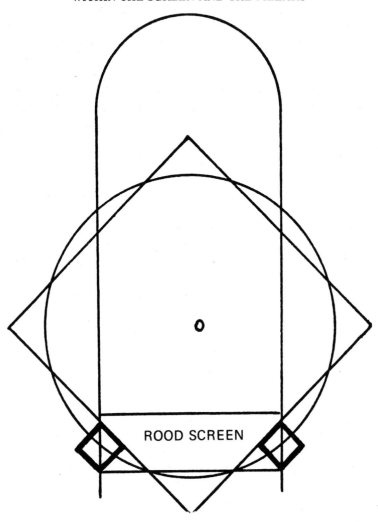

ROOD SCREEN

If one draws the round Table about the sacred centre, it cuts
extensions of the rectangular Table midway between the square
pillars of the crossbar (croisillon). The square Table drawn likewise
around the sacred centre determines the thickness of these pillars.
These two tables determine the area of the ancient screen (now
vanished) which bounded the base of the rectangular Table.

the choir and the crossing of the transepts. Its centre of construction coincides with that of the rectangular table, but not at all with the sacred centre, from which it is 2.523 metres away. Now, if you draw the round table round the sacred centre, its circumference, cutting extensions of the sides of the choir, will mark the siting of the pillars that bound the latter.

If one deals with the square Table in the same way, drawn with the sacred centre in the middle, the sides of the Table will indicate the thickness of the pillars.

Thus there is given not only a geometric solution, but a technical solution, since the thickness of the pillars is, technically, a function of the weight, height and thrust of the monument.

One may discern a coincidence in this. It is possible. I think myself, that the master-craftsman's *system*, at once very simple and very learned, was such that geometrical and technical solutions went together.

The screen, which closed the choir, was two fathoms and nine inches wide, approximately 4.20 metres. It is therefore likely that it filled the space between the pillars at the base of the rectangular Table.

It consisted of *seven* gothic arcades or galleries with pointed arches and was the only interior decoration in the cathedral. We know from some pieces that were found among the flagstones, of which some were stored in the crypt and others in the Louvre, with what admirable carving the screen was adorned.

The round-point also consisted of seven gothic 'arcades', refaced with great slabs of stucco during a century of light when men, Voltaire himself, condemned gothic as barbarous.

The round-point has this peculiarity that its axis is not exactly in line with the median line of the choir. The semi-circle inclines slightly to the north. This is not absolutely plain to the eye and only shews on the plan. To see a result of error in this would truly be to hold cheap

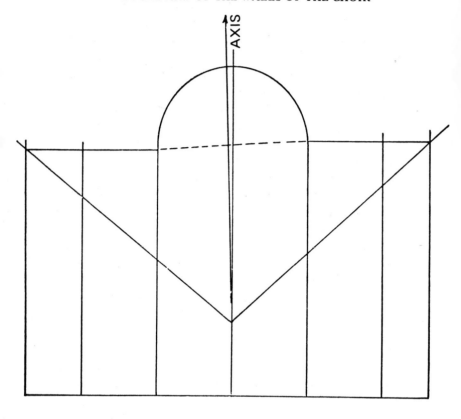

In consequence of the rotation to which the master-craftsman submitted the axis of the star with reference to that of the cathedral, there is a discrepancy between the width of the south and north aisles. Thus, the upper lateral points of the star do not cut the base of the round-point at the same level.

Theoretical calculation, based on a rotation of the axis of the star of one degree, which seems near enough to reality, gives a difference of nearly a metre between the widths of the two aisles, which corresponds with the fact and gives a distance from limit to limit of 47.04 metres; whereas mensuration gives 45.95 m as the width of the choir from wall to wall, a difference of 1.09 metres. As each main wall has approximately this thickness, the upper lateral branches of the star should have indicated the middle of the wall. We have no means of verifying this detail.

the knowledge that watched over the building of the monument; but the reason for it remains obscure. The cathedral replies, it is true; but to a question I do not know how to put.

Any more than I know how to put the questions that have to do with the irregular placing of the pillars on the south side of the choir and its aisle. The two pillars that frame the bay which contains the sacred Centre are further from one another than those of the other bays. While the average of the other bays is about 7 metres, the distance apart of these two is 7.83 m.

It is however to be noticed that this bay opens — opened before the tower of Jean de Beauce's choir was built in the XVth century — on the window of Notre-Dame-de-la-Belle-Verrière. Does the explanation lie here? Were they unwilling to restrict in any way the flow of light from this window?

The development of the seven-pointed star as the ruling principle of construction was not restricted to the choir only. It is the star that points to the limits of the second aisles.

If you prolong the line that marks the base of the round-point, it will be cut by the two upper lateral branches of the star at points which mark the walls of the choir at the middle of their base. Clearly because of the inclination, which I have just mentioned, of the semi-circle, there is a certain asymmetry between the north and the south walls. To my mind, this proves sufficiently that the inclination did not arise from error — which would have been spotted — but from a decision. Which has perhaps — I must stick to the *perhaps* so dear to Rabelais — some relation with the mysterious third quantity in the measurements of the cathedral.

At the points of junction between the two upper branches of the star with the base of the round-point, the apse begins, (likewise in accordance with a semi-circle centre on the centre of the round-point). But this

The apse is constructed on a seven branched star, in such a way that the centre of the chapel is not exactly on the axis of the cathedral. The directing circle of the ogive which has the same diameter as the distance from the walls of the choir, does not restrict but contains the centres of construction of the chapels, of which the interior measurement is 3.96 m. (5 Chartres cubits.) On the other hand these centres are marked by intersection of the bisections of the upper angle of the star incline.

semi-circle does not complete the apse, for it contains the centres of the three radiating chapels, whose inner radius is 3.70 m, a length we shall meet again in connexion with the second measure or quantity.

Before leaving the subject of the rectangular table, I will point out that from the beginning of the round-point to the base of the choir the distance is 26.32 metres; the width 16.40 metres. The proportions of this rectangle are very close to those of the Golden Number, which, for man, is the key-proportion of all aesthetics.

Until now I have used only the axes of the branches of the star. Now we must construct it. If you outline it by a circle passing through the 'points of the transept' which the builders used, it cuts the two lower branches at the height of the western end of the transepts, thus determining their width. Calculation indicates that this point should be 20.88 metres from the base of the choir. The measurement of the cathedral gives, for the width, 20.98 metres, a difference of 10 centimetres. Besides which, the circle drawn round the star, which allows us to construct this figure, cuts the two upper lateral branches at the angles of the containing towers at the junction of the walls of the choir and those of the semi-circle of the rounded apse.

Once again, geometrical construction solves a technical problem for the builder.

It remains to consider the 'public' part of the church; that is to say, the nave and its collaterals.

Its width is determined by that of the choir.

The width of the nave, plus the collateral aisles, from wall to wall, was determined by the diagonal of the square table.

As to its length, the sequence of the tables will give the necessary indications.

Next to the rectangular table, but separated from it by

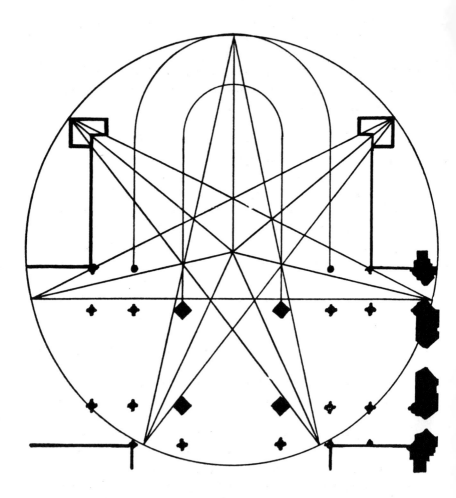

The form of the star gives a theoretical distance from the sacred centre to the base of the transepts of 31.10 m. Measurements give 31.083 m.

As for the towers that block the apse and the choir, it is clearly a question of the area.

THEORETICAL LENGTH OF THE TABLES

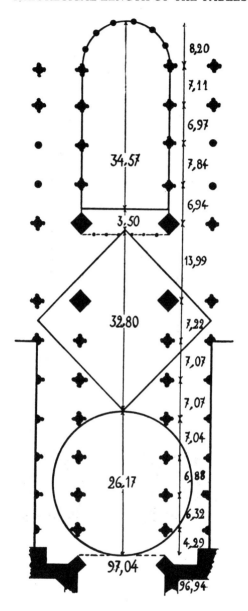

Giving various interesting measurements.

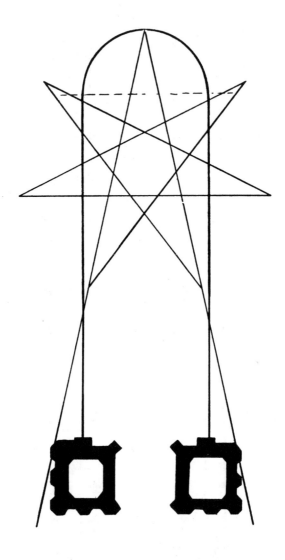

Although they were built fifty years before the Cathedral, the towers of the West front fit very exactly into the pattern defined by the star.

the screen, is the square table, its diagonal in the axis of the cathedral. And we find that the South-West angle of the square table is exactly over the white flagstone marked with a metal tenon on which, at the summer solstice the sun falls at noon on the day of Saint John.

In addition, one remembers that the surface of the square table was one hundredth that of the pyramid of Cheops; through the inclination of the cathedral this table, like the pyramid, has one of its faces almost exactly towards the true north. It is perfectly possible that when the table was indicated on the flagstones otherwise than by one single point — as is still the case at Amiens — it was not orientated with absolute exactness.

Let us put it that here is yet another coincidence.

Immediately after the square table comes the round table, which is fixed and befigured by the labyrinth which has fortunately been preserved. Of this more later.

Now, the circle of the round table, placed as it is next to the square table, *touches* the line that connects the eastern edges of the pillars that support the towers.

The initiatory way starts here.

In addition, if we· draw the star in the traditional form, that is to say, joining the points three by three, and if we prolong the sides of the highest point, which is in the axis of the cathedral, we notice that this angle encloses and delimits the western towers which were put in hand fifty years before the main fabric.

We shall understand why it seems so happy a coincidence that sited the towers where they are and gave them these dimensions.

14 The Grail and Alchemy

At this point, I may say, I was well satisfied with my little geometrical reflections, until I reminded myself that 'doors' do not open for no more than this.

I had gained the certainty that the master-craftsman of Chartres did not raise his cathedral on the basis of personal inspiration but by the application of traditional principles which could well belong to his calling.

Yet, the star, like the three tables, must answer some practical necessity. Whatever the Romantics may have thought, the great epoch of the cathedrals took no notice of Art for Art's sake. If there was to be anything symbolic it had to be both practical and vital.

Tradition says that three tables bore the Grail. What then was the Grail?

It appears, for us, in the Christian collection of Romances of the Round Table, in which it is a cup that was used by Jesus at the Last Supper and by Joseph of Arimathea thereafter to collect Christ's blood during the crucifixion. We are concerned then with a cup that contains the divine blood, poured into it directly or transmuted ('Drink. This is my blood . . .').

The quest of the Knights of the Round Table (here we have yet another table) was for the hidden cup, legend says; the cup that was kept in the Castle Adventurous of the Fisher King (we are now in the Piscean Age).

Moreover, the story of the Crusades shews that after the

capture of Ascalon a sacred cup fell into the hands of the Genoese, an octagonal gold cup: this is what gave birth to the legend of the Grail. Only, the Christian version is but an adaptation of a much older Celtic legend. And the word 'Grail' is itself Celtic.

Its origin is not for all that certainly Celtic. It may well be very much earlier. I believe that this word derives from the root 'Car', or 'Gar', which has the meaning of 'stone'. The *Gar-al*, or *Gar-el*, the urn that contains the stone or the stone urn (*Gar-al*), say, the Stone of God (*Gar-el*).

The two etymologies are in fact very close. In the first case, we should be concerned with a vessel in which the stone 'becomes'; in the second, with the 'Stone' itself. The symbol is unquestionably alchemical.

In practice we cannot separate the word 'Grail' from the word 'Cauldron'. In early Celtic times it was in the Cauldron (caldron) of Lug that 'universal medicines' were cooked over a special fire. Moreover, King Gradlon's name indicated that it was a guardian of the Grail who was engulfed in his town of Is when his Christian daughter Mahu destroyed the Menhirs that marked the fields.

Grail is a Celtic word; but one comes across the legend of the sacred cup under other names in other places and times. Melchisedek is represented in the north door of Chartres, known as the door of the Initiates, holding a cup that he hands to Abraham and from which the Stone protrudes.

Every Greek temple had its 'Krater' or cup, always with the radical *Cra, Car*.

Under whatever name, it invariably designates a vessel whose contents are taking their part of divinity; are penetrated with it; are in the process of transmutation.

One sees a very fine, Christian illustration of this on the wall of the church of Saint-Loup-de-Naud near Provins. Saint Loup stands there holding a chalice in which an emerald brought by an angel is materialising. The symbolism could hardly be clearer.

It is a question of alchemy. Alchemy, one knows, is the art and science of gathering, fixing and concentrating the vital current that bathes the worlds and is responsible for all life. It is a concentration that Adepts succeed in effecting, and which they establish on a supporting base: it is called the *Philosopher's Stone*. This stone works, because of the concentration, very powerfully and enables the Adept to bring about, in everything, an evolution that would otherwise take long centuries, if not millennia, to unfold in nature; notably — and this is the test — the metamorphosis of base metals into silver or gold.

But the vital current — the Spiritus Mundi, Spirit of the World, among alchemists works without check on everything in which it is bringing about evolution, man included. Good! Let it be admitted that in certain places, because of a 'concentration' of the vital stream, such evolutionary action may be stepped up; the more so as a man becomes 'receptive'; and it is this result, a kind of 'mutation' to use a fashionable term, that is sought and obtained in pilgrimage. Properly speaking, this is natural alchemy. Let it be admitted that the mode in which a man becomes receptive may affect the mode of his transmutation. And here the symbolism of the three tables is simply explained if in a summary and quasi-schematical manner.

As a man becomes himself in some sort the vessel, the Grail and its contents, three paths of approach to his 'mutation' are offered, represented and conditioned by the three tables; the round, the square and the rectangular, or, to speak in less allegorical style, Intuition, Intelligence, Mysticism. It goes without saying that we have here three manifestations, obvious, but inapprehensible by the senses, of human personality.

What relations are there between the three faculties and the tables, round, square and rectangle?

The round table appeared very early in the history of

humanity. Cromlechs, Fairy Rings, are round tables. One sees it in the Celtic Cross, which is enclosed in a circle. In a utilitarian sense, and provided always that it stands over certain surfacings of telluric currents, the round table resembles a ritual dance-floor, a floor for round dances that were a means of adaptation to natural rhythms.

It seems that the round dance, begun within the confines of the circle furthest removed from the centre, became for some a gradual approach to the centre in the measure that the rhythms possessed the man and freed him from the encumbrance of personality. In some fairy rings that were dance-floors three concentric tracks are found. It seems likely that a dancer who had arrived at a certain pitch of holy delirium had to end up with a gyration at the centre.

In some manner the dancer retraced the cycles of nature to their origin or, more unconsciously than consciously, found a way to get into direct relation with it. One can go further. A man who is revolving escapes from space. But to do this is also to go outside time. One may ask oneself to what extent a man who revolves in certain conditions becomes visionary. One thinks of the prophetic gifts of the Druidesses that shewed themselves in a sort of delirium during the dance. And of David dancing before the Ark and prophesying. And of the dancing Dervishes.

Let us also recall that round dances in the cathedral of Chartres, led by the bishop himself, were customary at Easter. Some see in this a representation of the movement of the stars: a thoroughly intellectual interpretation of a purely physical activity! Much more simply, it was a search for a state approaching the mediumistic which allows of identification with natural rhythms.

The round table was represented before Solomon's Temple by the Sea of Brass, in which there was water and whose prescribed measurements were, according to Abbé Moreus, in relationship with the weight of the Earth. The Templars, and not they alone, made a round table the centre of their churches. There they stood the altar.

To explain the square table asks for more subtlety. It is a 'squaring of the round'. It must give passage into the consciousness of instinctive knowledge: it is a table of intellectual initiation. It is very often depicted by a chessboard; and it is also the primitive child's game of Hopscotch, which was originally an abacus table, a work-table or a table of Numbers. It is moreover the table of Pythagoras, which is not merely a multiplication-table. Its most eloquent symbol, naturally, is the chessboard, which only the Queen and the Knight may cross in any direction mounted on the Mare, the 'cabala', knowledge.

It will be noticed that the tactic of the Cavalier or Knight makes use of the circle within the square, while Castles and Bishops can only move within their verticals or diagonals. This is a valuable indication. One does not stroll about among Numbers by virtue of the brain alone (unless it is merely a question of figures), any more than one makes music by adding note to note. What is indispensable is an initiation, at least instinctive, into the laws of harmony, natural law.

It is a trap on passing through which the intellect, left to itself, deludes itself regarding its own creations and is thus 'trapped' in its illusions as Bishop and Castle are caught between their lines of movement. To effect the squaring of the circle is to transform instinctive initiation into an initiation that is conscious, rational, active. For this one must mount the 'cavale', the cabala or traditional wisdom.

If I may push analysis a little further, I shall say that the square table has to do, not with life, but with organisation; it only assumes a real knowledge of matter. According to the ancients, the optimum organisation possible to society was founded on a squared plan that divided man into categories, or castes: the peasant who feeds, the soldier who defends, the craftsman who transforms, the trader who distributes; with degrees in each caste constituting a pyramid in three stages: apprentice, workman and master who, at the top, achieved Aristocracy, the true aristocracy of the Sage in his own class.

The square table is found again in the pyramid, in the Holy of Holies in the Temple at Jerusalem; and it is perhaps the basis of all the Templars' constructions, for the Order made copious use of the square in its commanderies or fortresses; joined what is more with a round church.

The rectangular table is mystical, a table of revelation. No explanation, no intellectual approach, is possible. It is the Table of the Last Supper, God's Sacrifice.

Here then is what can be said about the Grail and the tables. It is in no way astonishing that they present themselves in the order we have given, onward from the royal door, watched over by kings and queens who are now nameless. The succession fits well with the three births symbolically achieved in the covered way.

15 The 'Cubit' of Chartres

Let us return to our theoretical measuring chain.

Using this chain – on the ground plan it will be understood – one soon perceives that two intimately connected architectures have come together: one in stone, the other an architecture so to say of the void, having its own system of measurement, to which analysis of the immense fabric readily gives access. The figures themselves impose a preliminary statement.

In metres, the most 'notable' dimensions of the interior are close to the numbers 37, 74, 148.

The choir is approximately 37 metres long and 14.80 wide. The nave, with the same width, is about 74 metres long. The vault is 37 metres high.

A first working hypothesis can be established on these dimensions — or dimensions very close to them that the measures of length allow one to specify. For example, the length of the nave is twice that of the choir, and the total length of the main fabric (from the round-point of the choir — included — to the doors) is 110.76 metres (Merlet's figure).

Divided by three we get 36.92 metres.

The pillars of the main fabric, if you deduct the small pillars that surround them, have a diameter of 1.60 metres, so that the width of the invisible choir is 14.78 metres, or very nearly, four times 3.69 metres.

It would look, then, as if a measure very close to 0.369 metres was used, or, more likely, as regards the plan drawn on the ground, a length double that, simpler to use, 0.738 metres. For want of a better term we may call this the 'Cubit of Chartres'. Thus, we may draw up, in 'cubits', the following table of dimensions:

Width of the choir:	20 cubits
Length of the choir:	50 cubits
Length of the nave:	100 cubits
Length of the transepts:	90 cubits
Height of the vault:	50 cubits

We find this cubit again, what is more, in the thickness of the octagonal pillars (2 times), in the width of the towers (20 times), in the radius of the round chapels of the apse (5 times) and so on.

One cannot speak of coincidence in face of so systematic a usage. And we shall come across this cubit, or multiples of it, or simple fractions, in many other measurements.

What then is this cubit of 0.738 metres?

Quite simply, it is *the hundred thousandth part of the degree of the parallel of latitude of Chartres*. It is not I who say so but, on the one hand, a simple trigonometrical calculation based on what we know about the terrestrial radius and, on the other, a verification done on a 1/25,000 map of the National Institute of Geography.

Is this coincidence? Not the only one.

The Brotherhood that built Chartres cathedral signed its work in a way that I shall discuss further on. Their signature is to be seen on various monuments; at least on two of those whose essentials, restorers and other adapters to the taste of the day, have not destroyed: the cathedrals of Reims and Amiens. I have not had the opportunity to undertake a profound study of these two monuments, but, to confine myself to the only two bits of information that I possess, I note down the following.

Reims is situated at 49° 14' North latitude, which gives a degree of parallel of about 71 kilometres. The 'measure' or 'cubit' should therefore be 0.71 metres. The length of Reims cathedral is 142 metres and the interior length of the transepts is close to the geometrical mean between 71 and 35.5 metres.

Amiens is situated at latitude 49° 52', which would give a 'cubit' of about 0.70 metres. The height of the vault is sixty times 0.70 metres and the length of the transepts is 70 metres.

Clearly, it would be upsetting for them if you took from the men of today the illusion that they discovered the moon, whereas their ancestors, their eyes steadily fixed on the ground, looking for flints, did not notice it. The question must nevertheless be put: did the builders of Chartres know the terrestrial globe so well that they were able to choose for their work the measure best fitted to connect the harmony of the monument they had in hand with that of the terrestrial site where they were building it?

Two answers are possible. Either, the apparatus of measurement not being perfect at that time, we must admit that there exists in man means of knowledge, susceptible of extreme perfection, on which modern science has deliberately turned its back. And after all, it might seem as normal for a religious architect to discover the harmonic dimensions – the measure – for the place where he is working as for a musician to perfect a concord. Whether a science is intuitive or scholastic it is none the less science.

Or on the other hand, as I think myself, for reasons discussed above, the 'keys' to a system of knowledge, a system not lost but hidden, came into the possession of those who planned the building of cathedrals *via* the Order of the Temple, the Templars. *Archa Cederis*. You shall work by the Ark.

It will probably be objected that the figure of the degree

of parallel of Chartres is not 73.80 km but nearer 73.699 km. But this figure is itself inexact for we only have approximations as to the terrestrial radius and we do not know Earth's exact shape.

Moreover, measurements of the cathedral have not been made to the last millimetre and different measures are not completely agreed among themselves.

It is probable, if not certain (or this would be yet another coincidence!) that the absolutely exact unit of measurement used at Chartres was not 0.738 metres, but it is certain that it was very close to this figure.

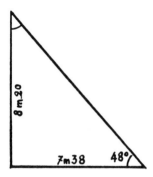

There are many other 'coincidences'. For example, the measure having served for the determination of the plan, 0.82 m and the cubit, 0.738 m are together in an astonishing relationship. Take a right-angled triangle in which one of the angles is of 48 degrees, the long side of the right angle is 0.82 m, the short side 0.738 m. And Chartres is very close to 48 degrees. We have at once the ratio of this parallel to its height over the equator.

Less astonishing is another coincidence. The Celtic well sinks to the water-table whose mean level is from 30 to 32 metres below the floor of the crypt: this gives us about 37 metres below the flagstones of the choir. The vault is about 37 metres above this floor. There is thus a correspondence between water and vault. And it is not without interest if one regards the cathedral as a musical instrument designed to amplify waves that have some sort of relationship with the underground current of water. For the cathedral is a musical instrument that makes use of resonances: this is certainly why its principal part is the emptiness, which constitutes its sound-box. All the master-craftsman's art and science went to the tuning with this emptiness, in quality, volume and tension, of the stone that gives it dimension.

To analyse the cathedral from this angle would be work for the lute-maker. Besides, it has already been noted that certain proportions on the ground had their equivalents in the intervals of a scale and that one would easily find in this the modes dear to Plato. Thus, it has been noticed that the length of the transepts is in the relation of a fifth with the length of the main fabric; that the total length of the nave is in the relation of an octave with the length of the choir; that the width of the nave is also in the relation of an octave with the width of the aisles.

These are the proportions that one comes across, plainly marked in the plan of elevation.

With this plan of a void, a resonance, overlapping the plan of the visible building, there should normally go three new tables which would no doubt be in harmonic relations with the numerical dimensions of the 'void'.

Such tables, in the great churches of the XIIth and XIIIth centuries, were marked out on the ground by arrangement of the flagstones but they have almost all disappeared. To· my knowledge, no rectangular table remains. A pavement, which has gone, should have given the outlines of such a table in the choir at Chartres. It is likely that an early altar stood at the centre, which was confused with the sacred Centre.

As to square tables, generally situated at the crossings of the transepts, it seems that only the cathedral at Amiens has kept one, repaired moreover, along with the whole stone floor of the church; but one may suppose it was copied from the original. Like that at Amiens, the table at Chartres must have been at the crossing and have had the same orientation as the table of construction: that is, its diagonal should have been identical with the axis of the cathedral.

A few round tables remain, among them those at Amiens and Chartres. At Chartres the table is indicated by black and white flagstones which outline a path that ends at the centre of a great white stone. It is called the Labyrinth. I shall have to return to the Labyrinth and its purpose.

What we know of the cathedral and the strict inter-dependence of all the elements of its construction makes one suppose it must have been the same with the tables and that there were dimensional relationships between the three.

Unhappily, as the tables at Amiens no longer have their original dimensions we are reduced, if we are looking for such relationships, to hypothesis, with the risk that these have no other value than guesswork.

Traditionally, the legend of the three tables is some-times told otherwise than as I have suggested. 'Three tables,' legend says, 'bore the Grail; one round, one square, the third rectangular. They have the same perimeter and their Number is 21.' Evidently, as with what legend says about the surfaces, we have here an enigma of which the builders held the solution in one form or another.

But even the bare mention of the Grail shews clearly that there is no question of trifling and that this 'trade-secret' had, in its application, an initiatory *signifi-cance and, especially in the case of a cathedral, a bearing on initiatory action.*

We must never lose sight of the fact that a cathedral was built for men, to work on them; and that everything to do with it was conceived with this object; that as Saint Bernard said, it was a *means.*

The fact that the remaining round table at Chartres may mark a path shews clearly enough that the 'second' tables were conceived in terms of length and not at all, as were the 'first' tables, necessarily, in terms of surface, since it was a question of determining the scope of the monument. It seems logical, then, to suppose that the second legend regarding the perimeters applies to the 'second' tables. Without doubt, surface and perimeter of the two sets of tables were in subtle relationships that it has not been given me to discover.

It is noticeable that these tables are centred on the axis of the cathedral and only occupy space that man can traverse. The round table in the nave, the square table at the crossing of the transepts, the rectangular table in the choir are in areas empty of all obstruction and entirely situated under the central vault.

At Chartres we now have only the round table: the Labyrinth. But it is sufficiently remarkable that a square with the same perimeter as the labyrinth should have for diagonal a length very near the width of the crossing of the transepts.

As to the rectangular table, a table with the proportions of 2 to 1, whose perimeter would be the same as that of the labyrinth and whose centre would coincide with the sacred Centre, its base should coincide very nearly with the limit of the old rood-screen. Which tends to confirm the hypothesis I suggested.

As to the problem of squaring the circle, there are several approximate geometrical solutions. One proceeds by way of the seven-pointed star; but this star, in this place, does not seem to be set in the plan of the monument. Another solution is that which traditionalists call 'the esoteric solution of the squaring of the circle'. Its basis is an analytic projection of the pyramid of Cheops. Unhappily this is an abstract pyramid. Perhaps it was once a real one; but the peeling off of its facing forbids us to state that it was thus and thus.

Yet another solution proceeds by the Golden Number, which may be geometrically constructed, as we have seen, on a rectangle with the proportions of 1 to 2. This gives, for the radius of a circle of the same perimeter as the square, half the side of the square multiplied by the root of the Golden Number: $\sqrt{}$ 1.618 = 1.272. This by the way, is the same solution as that given by the theoretical pyramid.

There is certainly an element of conjecture in the supposed relationship between the labyrinth and the square table in the crossing of the transepts, since nothing of the pavement that marked it remains.

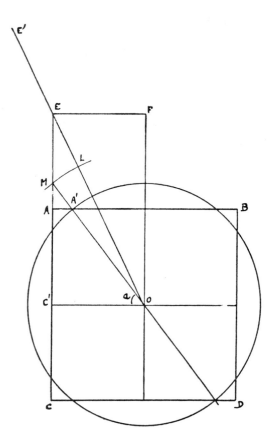

Suppose a square ABCD of which the side is AB = 2. Construct a rectangle C′EFO with width 1 and length 2. The diagonal OE is equal to $\sqrt{5}$. Prolong that diagonal of a length EE′ equal to EF. The length OE′ is equal to $\sqrt{5} + 1$. Take the half of that length OE^1, thus OL which is equal to $\dfrac{(\sqrt{5} + 1)}{2}$: which is the Golden Number 1.618.

Reduce the length OL to OM. OM cuts the side of the square, AB at A′. A′O is the radius of the circle whose perimeter has a value very close to that of the square ABCD. The radius A′O equal to MC′, has the value $\sqrt{1.618}$, or 1.272. Then angle (a) has the value $51^\circ\ 50'$

which is one of the angles of slope attributed to the pyramid of Cheops, which is not absolutely symmetrical. Metrically, the diameter of the labyrinth is given by the figure 12.87 m, but the 'useful' part of it, without the carved flower-work that surrounds it is given by 12.30 m, or a perimeter of 38.64 m. This supposes a square table with a side of 9.66 m and a diagonal of 13.66 m, and a rectangular table of 7.38 m, over 11.94 m, taking account, as must always be the case with lengths, of the relationship with the Golden Number. Now 7.38 m is twenty times the half cubit: 0.369 m.

16 The Musical Mystery

At 37 metres, a height imposed on them, the builders had to erect the widest gothic vault ever known, in harmonious proportions that had been worked out on the ground. The master-craftsman had clearly written the stagings of the 'lanceé' in four horizontal lines indicated by slight cornices. From base to the beginnings of the vault four stages surmount one another with diminishing solidity. At the top, the vault, pierced by high windows, seems to stand on nothing but slender, small columns of stone. The effective support of the flying buttresses is applied from outside the edifice.

Below there are massive pillars, alternatively round or octagonal, to which four slender columns, alternatively round or octagonal, are affixed, the octagonal to the round ones, the round to the octagonal. All are crowned with capitals, from which the ogives of the vault, the aisles and the 'formerets'* of the galleries spring. The tops of these capitals constitute the first horizontal.

Above them, at the base of the triforium, a light cornice makes the second horizontal.

A third horizontal cornice, above the galleries of the triforium, marks the base of the great twin windows

* The feature of an upright wall which takes the weight of an arch at the point from which it springs.

crowned with an eyelet in rose-colour. Finally, the line from which the vault springs is defined by a row of small capitals which constitutes the fourth horizontal.

The height of these horizontals above the floor of the choir can only be known approximately. The pavement has been restored and it is impossible today to ascertain the exact level of the earlier floor. It would therefore be impossible to undertake an accurate calculation in metres and centimetres unless approximation revealed in a formal manner that the measure employed was half the 'cubit', say, 0.369 metres. Figures, to this extent and without fractions, provide a certainty which the disappearance of the earlier pavement forbids to a modern system of measurement.

The geometry of the plan of elevation of the cathedral will be altogether musical.

The highest line, that of the small capitals at the root of the vault, is at 25.50 metres or about that. If, on a drawing of the vertical plan, the shape of the 'emptiness' of the fabric, one joins the high point to the angle of the base opposite, one gets with base and side, a right-angled triangle, one side of the right-angle being about 14.78 metres, the other 25.50. Calculate the length of the hypotenuse and you have a figure close to 29.50 m. Now twice 14.78 is 29.56. One may therefore allow, as a first hypothesis, that the hypotenuse is really 29.56 m, which would represent, geometrically an octave with a base of 14.78 m. The small capitals at the root of the vault should therefore be, not at 25.50 m but at 25.56 m.

In terms of the Chartres semi-cubit, the base would be 40 and the hypotenuse 80. A drawing on the ground, with measure and line alone, would give the height of the capitals at the root of the vault.

This right angled triangle is half an equilateral triangle. It is the 'divine triangle' of Plato and this Platonic observation leads to a search for modalities. If we seek the

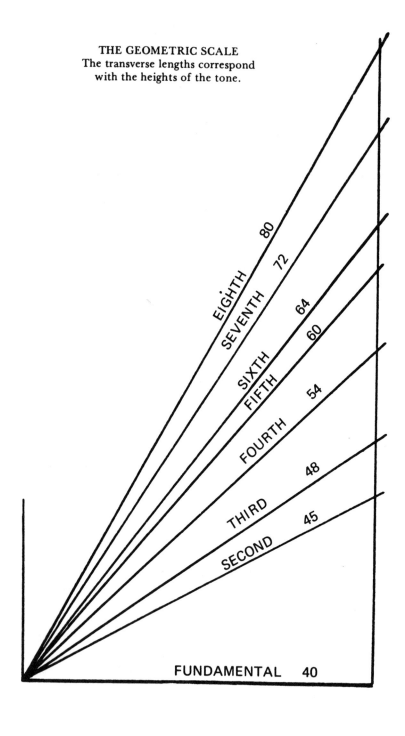

THE GEOMETRIC SCALE
The transverse lengths correspond
with the heights of the tone.

EIGHTH 80

SEVENTH 72

SIXTH 64

FIFTH 60

FOURTH 54

THIRD 48

SECOND 45

FUNDAMENTAL 40

arithmetical mean between two lengths 40 and 80, we get $(40 + 80)/2 = 60$. This is the interval of a fifth contained between 40 and 80. And if we now construct, according to the profile of elevation, a right-angled triangle with base 40 and hypotenuse 60, we obtain, on its side, a point situated at $\sqrt{60^2 - 40^2} = \sqrt{2000} = 44.72$. Or, $44.72 \times 0.369 = 16.50$. And 16.50 m is the height of the second horizontal line at the base of the triforium.

Fifth and octave. This leads us to a search for all the intervals of the scale.

It is known that the intervals in a scale are not equal but correspond with relationships, generally simple, between themselves and wholes.

By reference to a base frequency, and for a minor scale, these intervals, after analysis, are as follows:

For a second:	9/8
For a third:	6/5
For a fourth:	27/20
For a fifth:	3/2
For a sixth:	8/5
For a seventh:	9/5
For an octave:	2/1

Separating our basic note, geometrically, from our length 40, this is what we get:

For a second:	40 x 9/8	= 45 (16.60 in metres)
For a third:	40 x 6/5	= 48 (17.71 in metres)
For a fourth:	40 x 27/20	= 54 (19.92 in metres)
For a fifth:	40 x 3/2	= 60 (22.14 in metres)
For a sixth:	40 x 8/5	= 64 (23.61 in metres)
For a seventh:	40 x 9/5	= 72 (25.56 in metres)

If, separating one of the angles at the base of the

rectangle of elevation we carry the lines as hypotenuses, on the opposite side, we get, on this side, the following heights at the points of intersections:

For a second	(45)	20.612	(in metres: 7.60)
For a third	(48)	26.536	(in metres: 9.79)
For a fourth	(54)	36.276	(in metres: 13.38)
For a fifth	(60)	44.721	(in metres: 16.50)
For a sixth	(64)	49.96	(in metres: 18.43)
For a seventh	(72)	59.866	(in metres: 22.09)

The height of the capitals of the choir, 9.79 m, corresponds with the third; the height of the cornice under the triforium, 16.50, with the fifth; the height of the capitals at the base of the vault, 25.56, with the octave.

The second does not seem to have been indicated. It is possible that the fourth, 13.38 m corresponds with the height of the vault of the 'formerets'.

As regards the cornice at the base of the high stained glass windows, some doubt persists. No writer and no plan are precise about its exact height. In fact, it would seem that instead of utilising the interval 9/5 for the seventh, interval of a minor scale, the master-craftsman utilised 14/8, an interval of the major. A specialist in harmony would no doubt solve this little problem.

It would appear, in effect, after measurement and calculation that the length used was 40 x 14/8 = 70, in metres 25.83, which would put the height of the string course at 57.446, or, in metres, 21.19.

One is well aware that if the calculation seems a bit complex its realization in a drawing made on the ground will be most readily effected with line and measure, by simple addition of quantities in the sequence 40, 48, 60, 70, 80.

But in all frankness one must register a warning that the measurements of the elevation given by various authors being inexact, it is possible that another scale was used, which would upset the numerical relationships slightly, except for the 'tone' (or second) and the fifth, which are unchangeable.

It follows that the vertical growth of the cathedral, the stages of which are written in the horizontals, went in harmony with the width of the main fabric. This was itself in perfect harmony with all the other dimensions of the project, as we have seen. And the plan itself was in harmony with the place (the Mound and the water-table); with the parallel of Chartres. The place having the same speed of rotation as the Earth's crust, the distance covered in one hour is 1.107 kilometres. The length of the main fabric is 110.70 metres.

The vault too shares this harmonious growth and, what is more, introduces man to it. It is in fact constructed on the basis of a five-pointed star inscribed within a circle whose diameter is the height of the steeple. But, if we carry on with the idea of a geometrical scale as indicated by the heights of the 'horizontals', we find ourselves in a higher scale the length of whose base is double the octave of the first, as 'measured', 80.

The interval of a second is 80 x 9/8 = 90
The interval of a third is 80 x 5/4 = 100
The interval of a fourth is 80 x 27/20 = 108.

Now in the triangle thus formed on which 108 is the hypotenuse and the short side 40, the long side, that is to say the height, will be $\sqrt{(108)^2 - (40)^2} = 100.32$; or in metres 37.018, approximately the height of the vault. But the hypotenuse has another property — which we are unable to analyse, but the explanation and demonstration of it should not be beyond the skill of a good geometer — it cuts the circle in which the five-pointed star is inscribed at its lowest point, which is precisely a point of construction in the vault; centre of the arc of a circle that forms the half-curve opposite.

THE GEOMETRIC SCALE AT CHARTRES
WITH MEASUREMENTS IN METRES

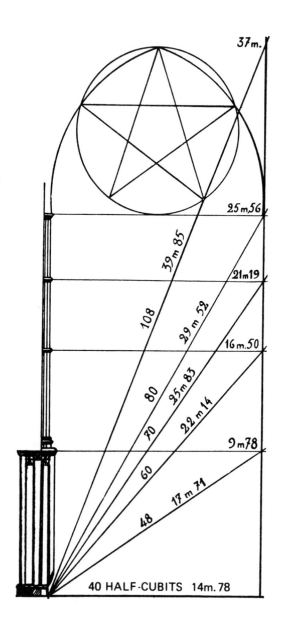

37 m.

25 m. 56

39 m 85

29 m 52

108

21 m 19

16 m. 50

35 m 83

22 m 14

80

70

9 m 78

60

17 m 71

48

40 HALF-CUBITS 14 m. 78

Thus, essential man finds himself incorporated in the general harmony and material structure of the cathedral. It will therefore be understood why we spoke of the cathedral as an agent of activity in man himself, in the sense of direct initiation and in the most natural way possible, with no empty theosophical jargon.

Note. Father Bescond, of Saint-Wandrille, writes to me, on the subject of the musical development of the elevation:

I think I have found the answer to the harmonic problem: the scale is neither major nor minor; it is the scale of the earlier Gregorian mode, based on RE. The 'good notes' of this mode are RE-FA-LA.

In addition, the distribution of the notes constitutes:

first, in nave and choir, up to the vault,

RE-FA, first third, minor harmonic 6-5;

FA-LA second third, major harmonic 5-4 (the LA is lowered by a comma);

LA-DO third third, the so-called 'minim', 7-6 (the DO is depressed).

Three different thirds (3 x 3, sacred figures).

The interval RE-DO is *the* 7th Harmonic 7-4; it is thus also *the* 7th harmonic emitted by the fundamental RE (7, sacred figure) (RE gives the harmonics RE^3, RE^4, LA^4, RE^5, FA^5, LA^5, DO^6;

The three thirds and the seventh are crowned by the octave (a new sacred figure);

If one inserts the SOL (27-20) in the scale, it divides the third FA-LA into two unequal tones, the major FA-SOL = 9-8; the minor SOL-FA = 10-9.

So that if you align all the harmonic relationships of this scale you get the following series:

10-9	9-8	8-7	7-6	6-5
SOL-FA,	FA-SOL,	DO-RE,	LA-DO,	RE-FA,

5-4	4-3	3-2	2-1
FA-LA,	$LA-RE^4$,	RE^3-LA,	RE-RE

The measures projected are 40, 70, 80; sacred numbers, and 4 x 12 = 48, and 5 x 12 = 60, sacred numbers.

The place of DO is unusual enough, it is true, and seems never to be used in the Gregorian chant; all the same, this note appears in the musical theory of Safi-ud-Din (Dervish-Turkish writer in Arabic towards 1250, which is late with reference to Chartres; but he did not *invent* the seventh harmonic — he was the first witness known to hold it in honour, which seems to imply that it had acquired citizen's rights in the tradition of his time).

As to the vault, this is constructed on the Fourth (4 is the mystical figure of man, in opposition to Three, mystical figure of God) and the five-pointed star (same symbolism). The Fourth 27-20 is not the usual Fourth (4-3); it is a little higher and is called the 'intense fourth'. With the LA it makes a seventh, different from the RE-DO; it is the 'brilliant seventh' = 9.5.

One would never come to an end of underlining the harmonic relationships between different measures; all coherent and all simple, never two of them the same.

17 The Mystery of the Light

We must now explore a particularly mysterious region and one that has so remained because traditional science wills it: the region of light. Robert Grossetête (1175-1253) said of it that its beauty was 'due to the simplicity with which light is in unison with music, more harmoniously linked with itself in a relationship of equality'.

The stained-glass window is light.

The gothic stained-glass window, for ever unexplained, for ever inexplicable, lasted throughout the age of 'true gothic'. Master and servant of light, whose effect comes less from the colour of its mosaics or fragments of glass than from a certain unanalysable quality of both colour and glass.

For as a fact this glass does not react to light like ordinary glass. It seems to be transformed into a precious stone that does not so much let the light pass as itself become luminous.

Under the harsh and direct action of the sun, a stained glass window does not project its colour as does merely tinted glass, but only a diffused, clear splendour. Another peculiarity is that whether the light outside the church is soft or harsh the window is just as splendid and even remains as luminous in the shades of twilight as in full day. No chemical analysis has so far, to our knowledge, penetrated the mystery of the gothic window.

It has been claimed that this luminosity and its inimitable colours are due to an 'irisation' of the glass from without brought about by the elements. This is manifestly wrong, for one remarks none of these qualities in the stained glass windows of the XIVth century, all of them just as accessible to this process of 'irisation' as those of the XIIth and XIIIth.

For the 'true' stained-glass window appeared suddenly in the first quarter of the XIIth century and vanished towards the middle of the XIIIth. Just like gothic itself.

After the middle of the XIIIth century, men can still build on the crossed ogive and even push the technique to astounding lengths of virtuosity, but it is no longer anything but that. Man the architect expresses himself in stone, but it is no longer the Word. The glazier may paint his bit of glass with the highest skill, but it will never be anything more than painted glass.

The stained-glass window and true gothic are inseparable. Like true gothic, the window is a product of high science, a product of alchemy.

The conformist attitude of today demands that we regard alchemy with some condescension, as the vestige of a proto-chemistry still in its infancy. This arises because the knowledge of it was kept secret; in part because of the danger of putting certain skills in the wrong hands; in part, above all, because what was in question was a very complex science of the highest philosophical significance and because it could not be learnt by itself. But however this may be, it is safe to assert that the builders of Chartres were no more ignoramuses than were the chemists who made the windows apprentices in a laboratory. The product of their knowledge, builder and glazier, is open to all and sundry — and visible.

These windows attest, from green to black, black to white, white to blue, from blue to purple and purple to gold, the transmutation of matter by the fire of the sun and by fire celestial. The colours achieved in these windows, moreover, according to sages who practised the ancient Hermetic science, are those which were seen during the development of the Great Work.

Listen now to what a Hermetical of the XVIth century, the Sancelrien Tourangeau, wrote:

'Our stone has two more very surprising qualities. The first, with regard to the glass, to which it imparts all sorts of interior colours. as in the windows of the Sainte-Chapelle at Paris and in those of thy churches of Saint-Gatien and Saint-Martin in the city of Tours . . .'

True stained-glass appeared in Persia towards the XIth century. It came from the laboratories of certain Adepts among whom we should mention the mathematician and philosopher Omar Khayyam, poet of the Rubayyat, poet of the rose, product of a mutation brought about by these same Alchemists.

It was seen in the West at the same time as gothic, that is, in the first quarter of the XIIth century — and there is plenty of room for the supposition that it had the same origin — scientific documents deposited with the Cistercians by the first nine Templars.

In the care of the Cistercians, in their abbeys of Obazine and Pontigny, one may see windows which are, Régine Pernoud says, *true miracles of technique and art. The glass is white, or rather uncoloured, in principle; but in practice the glaziers knew how to make a sort of translucid paste with the unaided resources of their cooking and in various thicknesses as the paste rose, a glass with a pearly light that would itself put an end to our regrets over the triumphant colours in other windows.* *

The coloured window appears at Saint-Denis after repairs were made to the basilica in gothic style; and for a time *all* windows of this quality, the work of an unknown Adept, are gifts from the Abbot Suger. Such was the stained-glass window to the glory of Our Lady that he presented to Notre-Dame at Paris and which a slave-bishop caused to be smashed in the XVIIIth century because it did not let in enough light.

* Régine Pernoud: *'Les grandes époques de l'Aet en occident'* (Ed. du Chêne).

It is very likely that Notre-Dame-de la-Belle Verrière came from Saint-Denis. And the great western windows: the Tree of Jesse, the Triumph of the Virgin and the Life of Christ.

As to this, Suger, no doubt overloaded with requests for the products of his workshop, wished to demonstrate how glass was stained in his Abbey. And many a spagyrist or glazier tore his hair out in despair.

With the building of gothic churches the centre of the window-making technique moved to Chartres. Windows from that town were to be seen in Paris, Rouen, Bourges, Sens. They are often signed Clément de Chartres, without it being possible to know whether we are talking about the Adept who stained the glass or the Master Glazier who designed and assembled the window, which is more likely as Adepts usually remain anonymous.

It seems however that towards 1140, when all the windows at Chartres were in place, the 'source' of stained glass began to dry up, probably through the Adept's disappearance, his work being finished.

Let us go a little further into the mystery.

Light, if we are to believe both tradition and modern science, is a combination of two things: on the one hand, luminous vibrations and, on the other, a particle of energy. This, in the sun's light, is active, penetrating, sterilising and relatively dangerous to life; human bodies defend themselves against it by a process of pigmentation which is strongly the fashion today. Its action is such that no alchemical experiment can be attempted in the light of day; no more than the experiment in human alchemy which is initiation. As alchemists seek protection from the sun's light for their work at the furnace, so initiation requires the protection of cavern or crypt.

It is for the same reasons that sabbath dances are performed at night and not at all for reasons to do with diabolism invented for their own purposes by the Inquisition, after Albert the Great and Thomas Aquinas.

Jesus was born at night, in a cavern, not in full daylight. 'The Lord said that he would dwell in the thick darkness,' declared Solomon (I Kings, viii. 12).

It was not for the simple purpose of disguise that early Masses were said in caverns or catacombs, then in crypts, then in temples of stone that reproduced the crypt above-ground. This was done in all religions anterior to Christianity. The Greek mysteries were enacted at night.

Nor was it for technical reasons that romanesque churches were no longer open to the light — romanesque walls could be pierced with as many apertures as it might be wished without damaging their solidity. A large number have no opening on the choir but a domed niche over which a curtain could be drawn as in Solomon's Holy of Holies. The chapels of the Command-posts, reserved to the Knights Templar, had no opening. And let us recall the obligatory night-office in most of the monastic Orders.

One may then ask oneself whether alchemical glass, endowed with strange properties that it exposes to the light, does not constitute a filter which while it lets the luminous vibrations through, retains the particle of energy that is harmful to the evolution of man within the Temple.

And one may ask oneself whether the leaded 'glass of antimony', of romanesque churches was not a first experiment in this direction.

Let us advance still further.

Alchemists hold that the 'staining' that colours the material in the fabric of the Great Work is due to incorporation of the Spiritus Mundi which bathes the universe. When one remembers what influence simple commercial colours exert on man's mind and behaviour, what power must this glass possess raying on the man whom it bathes?

Was it not recommended at Chartres itself that the men

who were setting certain windows should be telling their beads? Recital of the litany depersonalised a man while the colour-harmony of the Spiritus Mundi replenished him.

Moreover, direct homage is paid in the cathedral at Chartres, as in every Notre-Dame, to Alchemy: in the rose-windows or rosaces — we are not called on to detail the operational symbolism — and in the lancets below the Rose over the North door (also known as the Gate of the Initiates). There we may see famous Adepts of the Old Testament gathered about a Saint Anne with black face who carries a fleur-de-lys:

Melchisedek, the Chaldean magus who hands to Abraham the sacred cup which is the Grail;

Aaron, the Egyptian magus, 'brother' of Moses, who erected the Golden Calf in the desert;

David, musician-king, inspired by the Ark that contained the Tables of all knowledge.

Solomon, builder of the Temple of Jerusalem, 'wiser than Moses and full of all the wisdom of Egypt', who left after him, under the title of Song of Songs, his book of Adeptship.

One has felt astonishment over the colours in the windows at Chartres and the harmony that governs their composition. How could it be otherwise when the Spirit of the World itself decided them? How could they fail to harmonise with the vessel of geometrical and musical harmony that Earth and Sky planned and projected?

People were astounded to learn, in the middle of the last century, that in other times glaziers ranked as gentlemen and were allowed to carry a sword. They concluded that it was a case of gentlemen who qualified as glaziers. The truth is very different. It was the art of window-making that ennobled them as students of the Great Work. This was the true nobility of philosopher or Adept and the external sign of such a chivalry could only be conferred by an Order of Knighthood.

One can, I suppose, be certain that the Master Craftsmen

of the Children of Solomon likewise carried a Knight's sword, Horsemen as they were of the *Cavale*, the *Cabale*. Besides, a sword is used for 'testing' stone.

Again, the *Compagnons des Devoirs* possessed each one of them a personal paper on which was written, in hieroglyphs, what you might call his qualification, from the point of view of his trade as well as his esoteric knowledge. This paper, which served as passport in the 'cayennes', they called their 'Horse'. In reality it was their armorial bearings as members of an Order of Chivalry, 'Cabalerie'.

When a companion died his 'Horse' was burnt in the course of a secret ceremony. The ashes were mingled with wine and the companions drank it. To move to some other place, in certain circumstances, was to be *en cavale*, that is, under the protection of the cabale or in its service.

Not all the windows at Chartres are alchemical. A good part of them were destroyed, notably those high up in the choir, by a bishop who wished to be seen in full daylight. He deserves to go down to posterity as Omar the Incendiary. He summoned Bridan and had sixteen of these windows smashed, in 1773 and 1778. He by himself certainly did more damage at Chartres than the Huguenots and revolutionaries.

This following the destruction of the rood-screen in 1763 by order of the chapter.

18 The Companions

The cathedral at Chartres was built by specialists. Workers in gothic style, builders of churches, *Workmen*. They left their signature on the stones they shaped, on the beams they assembled, signs that are their mark. We know almost nothing else about them. Their origin is mysterious and has become legendary.

A legend is created with the object of handing something on to those who have the key to its understanding; but sometimes the key is lost and the tale forgotten. Legend alone remains. To seek history in a legend opens the door wide to error. Legend is sometimes extremely clear; sometimes it is less so and one must have recourse to hypothesis.

It is known that the builders of churches were united in fraternities, brotherhoods or guilds. Of brotherhoods there were three — *The Children of Father Soubise, The Children of Master Jacques* and *The Children of Solomon.* They have not totally disappeared; they left heirs who are known now as *Les Compagnons des Devoirs du Tour de France,* a title given them in the XIXth century. Some of them seem to have observed a tradition of initiation, some not; but all observe a tradition of their calling, a moral tradition of chivalry within their craft and submission to work that *must* be done.

A tale is current regarding them.

Three men were at work in a stone-yard. A passer-by asked them, 'What are you doing?'

'I'm earning my bread,' said the first.

'I'm following my trade,' said the second.

'I'm building a cathedral,' said the third. He was a Companion.

Etymologically, companions are men who eat the same bread. But this etymology is not the only one. For Raoul Verges, companions are men who know how to use a pair of compasses.

Those who share the same bread form a community, a brotherhood; those who know how to use a pair of compasses are men who have been admitted to the knowledge of certain geometrical laws of harmony that permits them to attain the status of 'workman'. (Spelt *œuvrier* in the French text.)

Pursued, at the time of the trial of the Templars, by Philippe le Bel's officers, banned by the corporations, they took the title *Compagnons des Devoirs* and put on the cloak of secrecy, never to discard it until the French Revolution, when the corporations were destroyed. They recognised one another by words, signs and a private language of their trade. The word *devoirs* had its own meaning for them: the duty of work, which in old days was laid on them with the means of doing it. Their traditions are deep-rooted and are expressed at the 'trade' or craft level in a hierarchy of three degrees, apprentice, companion and attained-companion or Master. On the human plane, as those who have vital work to do, they refused, until the obligation became formal, to bear arms and as Knights, which is to say liberators, they have always refused to work on the building of fortresses and prisons. They refuse it, I think, today.

I think I do not betray them if I say that their basic thought is that man is *worth* what he is capable of doing. Not very pleasing to modern syndicates or trades unions.

Apprentices learnt their trade moving from yard to yard in the course of a *Tour of France*, under the direction of companions or some other; but the knowledge peculiar to their brotherhood was taught them privately, in *cayennes*, by masters.

The three fraternities, which sometimes fought among themselves, are today united in one single association; but it would seem that in the beginning their 'duties' and techniques were different.

The *Children of Father Soubise* was founded by a legendary Benedictine (but a wood belonging to a Benedictine monastery near Poitiers still bears his name). It was he who instructed the companions. It is likely that it was a fraternity set up in the very heart of the Benedictine monastic system where 'laymen' engaged in the trade were taught and where, in those times, they enjoyed the necessary protection of the monastic houses whose habit they wore — or did not.

And because the romanesque style is Benedictine I tend to believe that it was this fraternity, the Children of Father Soubise, who with the aid of builder-monks built romanesque churches and cathedrals. At the time when the fraternities were subjected to persecution, in the XIVth century, they refused to separate from the Church.

Another companionate fraternity was that of the *Children of Maître Jacques*. They became the *Compagnons Passants du Devoir*. Their legend is full of poetry.

Their founder would be a Maître Jacques who was born in a little Gaulish town called Carte (now Saint-Romilly*) in the Midi. His father was the master-craftsman Jacquin, created Master after his journeys in Greece, Egypt and Jerusalem, where he made the two pillars of the Temple of Solomon of which one is actually called Jacquin.

They are 'passants'. I tend to think that this is not a participle of a reflexive verb but designates men who 'gave passage'. And when one knows what obstacles rivers so

* Lucien Carny, in Atlantis No. 222.

long presented to passengers, one can imagine that to organise their passage, perhaps by ford, perhaps by throwing up bridges, would constitute an important work of co-operation in the civilising process. Perhaps they were the heirs of those *Moines Pontifes* who were great bridge-builders. Unless indeed they preceded them, for their legend goes far back, like the name Jacques itself which for long designated the Gaulish peasant. It is admissible, then, that the Children of Maître Jacques were the successors to that confraternity of Celtic builders who signed their work with an oakleaf.

Finally, one may suppose that they constituted a brotherhood whose task was to organise religious facilities and accommodation on the road to Saint-Jacques-de-Compostella.

It is to the third brotherhood, the *Children of Solomon*, that I would readily attribute the building not only of Chartres but a good part of the gothic *Notre Dames* and, in any case, for they seem to me to be 'signed', those at Reims and Amiens. For the following reasons:

The *Children of Maître Jacques* seem to have lived, at least until they became clandestine, in Aquitaine. Their churches, decorated with the *chrisme à l'épee*, or with a cross of Celtic appearance, enclosed in a circle, are only come across with rare exceptions in the South of France. They have moreover a highly personal style.

The *Children of Father Soubise*, Benedictines, seem dedicated rather to the romanesque; and the brotherhood signs of the builders of romanesque differ widely from those of the builders of gothic, even when their work is contemporary. And as there was necessarily a brotherhood of gothic builders it can only be the *Children of Solomon*. Besides, it is with their successors, the *Compagnons du Devoir de Liberté*, that there rests the tradition of instruction in the indispensable descriptive geometry, the 'Trait', by the Cistercian monks. In this case there would have been created at Citeaux a fraternity of religious

THE 'CANTONNED' PILLAR

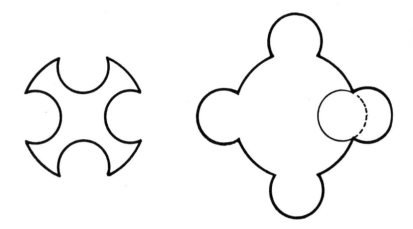

The inversion of a Celtic cross; the basis of the 'cantonned' pillar.

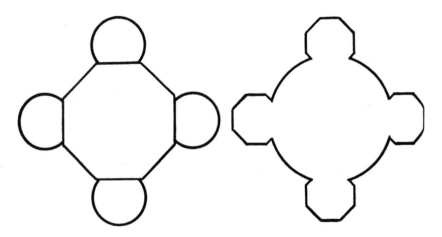

The two resolutions of a 'cantonned' pillar as found at Chartres.

builders on the same lines, if you like, as the Order of the Temple, to whom their protection would have been confided until immunity was acquired.

The name of Solomon itself might well be a supplementary indication. Solomon, Adept, caused the Temple to be constructed and buried the Ark in it. Saint Bernard, Cistercian, found himself under obligation to unfold, in one hundred and twenty sermons, the Adept Solomon's Song of Songs. Saint Bernard created the Order of the Temple whose first name was *Templum Salomonis,* or Solomon's Temple. The Cistercians instructed the *Children of Solomon.*

Let us add that it was at the request of d'Amaury, Prior on behalf of the Gauls in the Temple — he was linked with them in friendship — that Saint Louis accorded to the lay fraternities of church-builders immunities which dispensed them from the necessity of other protection.

A question remains to be asked. What were the conditions of coexistence with the Order of the Temple? Were they *within* the Order, or merely affiliated, or associated?

It is difficult to answer this, for the Temple had a very complex organisation, a mixture of monks and laymen, soldiery and craftsmen, all 'brothers'. At the base were the Brothers of the monastery who, men-at-arms or not, were *monks,* having made their vows. These were the true Templars. Within the general organisation there were also volunteers, serving for life or for a time, among them Brothers of the craft who could equally well have been builders belonging to the Children of Solomon. One sees how difficult it is to answer our question.

All the same there is one indication. In the command-posts the Knights lived in a reserved building forbidden to women which only those who were invited might enter. This was the Great House, the Convent properly speaking. The Great House is obviously so called by contrast with a

Little House. Now in Gallic, preserved in the Caux country and no doubt in Picardy, the little, the small, is the *cayenne*. And the *cayenne* is traditionally a place reserved to the fraternity of builders. It may therefore be logically admitted that there existed, alongside the great Order of Knights of the Temple of Solomon a minor Order that was affiliated in some manner with the great Order — the *Children of Solomon.*

In any case, at the same time as he staged the trial of the Temple, Philippe le Bel suppressed the immunities granted to the masons. If the *Children of Father Soubise* bowed to this, not so the *Children of Solomon* who, after creating a certain amount of trouble, went into hiding or, many of them, expatriated themselves. Considering themselves absolved of all obligation to the King of France and the Papacy, guilty of not having defended the Order, they became Foreign Companions of the *Devoir de Salomon.*

Need we take account of certain coincidences between the signature of the Brotherhood that built the various Notre-Dames and certain buildings of the Templars?

The Brotherhood, especially at Chartres, Amiens and Reims, seem to have signed their work with the systematic use of the 'cantonned' pillar. This was certainly not their invention: one comes across it in many romanesque buildings; but something special about its proportions characterises it in some manner. The column is round or octagonal (Chartres), but the columns that 'canton' or surround it (in the pattern of a cross) present the peculiarity that, with reference to the main columns, they have the same proportion as the small circles that cut the central circle bear to the Celtic cross.

As well as in Amiens, Reims and Chartres, we find this signature, which could be that of a School, in two of the pillars of Notre-Dame in Paris, near the west door, and two at Beauvais, one in each transept.

Without wishing to draw hasty conclusions, one is led,

in spite of oneself, to compare these pillars with the classic keep of the Templars, the tower 'cantonned' with four turrets, such as may still be seen at Sarzay, Indre, or even with the keep at Vincennes, a copy of the *Temple Tower* in Paris. There is also some relationship with *Caesar's Tower* in Provins, probably the work of the builders who built the fortresses of the Temple. The relationship between the octagonal and the round pillars leaps to the eye.

There are yet other pointers. At Reims, Amiens and Chartres, at the Royal entrance, in embrasures in the vaulting, two knights — sometimes naked as at Reims — stand behind a single shield of carbuncle. Is this to recall the Templar duality? The Carbuncle is an alchemical symbol.

Other historical coincidences offer themselves. True gothic, born at the same time as the Temple, comes to an end with it. Gothic becomes the 'ogival', the 'flamboyant'; mere virtuosity, no longer initiatory. Seemingly the stained-glass window disappears, and gives way to painted glass that is worth less than the paint and has no other value than whatever charms it may possess.

Are we then to conclude that those who conceived these monuments, the 'sages', found themselves in the Temple and disappeared with it?

19 The Treasure of the Temple

We must go further. There is room for the question, not only whether the men who built the Notre-Dames were protégés of the Temple but also whether these churches, the cathedral at Chartres in particular, were not one of the charges given to the Order by Saint Bernard.

Before the Temple the only great churches were Abbeys. Secular or laic churches were small. The church of Fulbert at Chartres, which however was far from having the development of the cathedral itself, is an exception. Notre-Dame in Paris occupies the space of three earlier churches; and Paris was already a great city.

We must look at things as they were. Most French towns, to the north of the Loire, were but small boroughs with extremely limited means. Money was scarce and did not circulate. When a community possesses something, or can get hold of it, the first thing it undertakes in the way of building concerns the walls that give it relative security from incessant warfare and the plundering bands that have no more respect for open cities than the regular troops. Such towns have only small churches and they are without the means to build great ones. If absolutely necessary, in rich towns like Rouen, second city in the kingdom, they multiply the number of parishes and decorate the churches in them, thanks to gifts from one source or another.

How then, in a few years and in all of them at the same time, from Paris to petty boroughs of some few thousand inhabitants, did they find the money required for the

1307, no document now remains on the uses to which it was put, otherwise than the victualling of the Army of the East. But in Spain, on the dissolution of the Order, the knights entered the Order of Calatrava in large numbers; and it seems very likely that Christopher Columbus, who stayed there, discovered in the monastery of Calatrava grounds for his conviction regarding the existence of the West Indies.

In Portugal there was created, following the dissolution of the Order of Knights Templars, and especially for them, the Order of Christ, which bore the red cross of the Knights (*la croix templière, la croix de gueules pattée* – there must be a recognised English description); and when the Portuguese with Henry the Navigator, Grand Master of the Order of Christ, threw themselves into the task of discovering oceans, with an air of knowing perfectly well where they were going, they were obliged to stamp their sails with the cross of the Order of Christ, in other words the cross of the Order of Knights Templars.

But Jean de La Varende, who has had in his possession a number of historic documents belonging to old Norman families, makes one of his characters say regarding the 'Gentlemen', that the Temple went looking for gold from the Mexican mines, and that this money was then concentrated at Sours, 'our command-post near Chartres'.

But money, rare until towards 1100, became more plentiful towards the end of the Middle Ages and during the Renaissance. Where did it come from? The German mines were then unknown, those of Gaul exhausted or lost, the Russian ones still unprospected. We have here perhaps the secret of the building of Chartres, so well done, so quickly, so easily. And not only Chartres.

I bring forward no direct proofs. As regards the Temple, there never were any. Documents, if they existed, have never been recovered. The sole proof is the absence of contrary possibilities.

I hold that the Temple was responsible for the building

of the great Gothic cathedrals, for the good reason that no other organisation could possibly have enabled bishops and chapters to realise such projects.

As to Chartres, it is only by its direct intervention that we can explain how the master-craftsman and his corps of carpenters, stone-cutters, sculptors, quarrymen, masons, could have come so quickly on the scene after the fire of 1194. It is only by its intervention that we can explain how the entire plan, except the porches, added later, came to be carried out in twenty-six years.

Was not this the charge laid on them by Saint Bernard? They were Knights and a Knight's mission is to succour and deliver.

We will recapitulate.

When they appeared in Palestine, what did they put forward as their mission, even if it was only a blind? To protect and deliver pilgrims from robbers who stripped them as they went on their way.

What did they do in Europe? They organised cultivation, This, on the one hand, is to deliver peoples from the hunger that raged, sometimes with extreme severity; on the other hand to rescue serfs and peasants from the arbitrary proceedings of lords and bishops. They did indeed employ serfs in their own demesnes, but such as could hardly have deemed themselves specially unfortunate when one calls to mind the *bourgeoises*, women in easy circumstances, with the property qualification, who married serfs of the Temple at Provins.

They protected travellers, pilgrims and merchants on the roads under their surveillance. They delivered them from highwaymen, lords and cut-throats; from tolls also and other taxes levied by certain land-owners.

In their enclosed stations there lived, beyond attack, numerous craftsmen: weavers, smiths, wheelwrights, masons and so forth.

It was they who obtained from King Saint Louis royal immunities for the church-builders and their brotherhoods.

They did nothing that was not directed to improvement of the human lot, protection of the weak, deliverance from slavery or injustice – you will reign in the measure that you are just, said a prior of the English Temple to king Henry. The sword was only bestowed on you for the defence of the weak and the poor, said Saint Bernard to Thibaud of Champagne.

It is then a question of the promotion of human welfare; and this would be incomplete without Temples of initiation acting directly on the individual to awaken in him the spirituality without which a man is never complete.

It was impossible to dissociate themselves from the building of such a temple, in a place held in reverence by one and all, at Chartres where Mother Earth pours forth her ineffable gift.

And then, we have an astonishing fact.

Apart from the carved screen, there was no sculpture within the cathedral at Chartres.

The chapel of Saint-Piat dates from the XIVth century. The bishops had it built at the end of the rounded apse, that is to say, outside the monument itself, to serve them as a burial-place since the ground beneath the cathedral was prohibited. The Vendôme chapel dates from the XVth century and it is a catastrophe. The 'tower of the choir' was begun in the XVIth century by Jean de Beauce, when he had finished the spire of the North Tower on the western face. It is clear that immense pains were taken to deaden in no way the resonance of the building. One does not hang ornaments on a harp string.

Decoration, the carved figure, which was a kind of historical or symbolical teaching, was reserved for the exterior and more especially the porticos and great doors. This too was sometimes an 'explanation' of the building and its place in Christendom in the widest sense of the phrase 'Christian civilisation'.

However, over the Royal Door, the central tympanum was decorated with an admirable Christ in Glory surrounded by four evangelical symbols. There is an Ascension of Christ on the left-hand door. On this same portico, carved on the capitals that surmount the columnar figures of what one thinks must be kings and queens of Judah, there is told in little scenes full of life and movement, the story of Mary and Jesus. It is remarkable that in thirty-eight scenes not one represents the crucifixion.

One goes straight from the Kiss of Judas to the burial. There is no mention here of the cross and its suffering.

Thus also with the other two great doors, which date from about 1220 to 1240. The same also with the porches that were built before 1260.

The Christ is at the south entrance, on a pier of the central door, teaching and blessing. He is seen in the tympanum of the door on the right, between Mary and John. He stands between two angels at the door on the left, the door of the Knights. There are some other scenes from the life of Jesus at the North door; but nowhere a Christ crucified. (I believe it is the same at Reims and Amiens, in those parts of the cathedral that are earlier than the XIVth century).

There is in the great stained-window-work on the west side in the space consecrated to the life of Jesus — to the left as one enters the cathedral — a small medallion shewing Christ on the cross; but we have here one of the windows of the XIIth century which probably came from Saint-Denis. And one remembers that the Templars refused to admit that the man Pilate crucified was really Christ. This, at the time of their trial and in spite of the little faith one has in declarations obtained under torture by Dominican inquisitors, was their constant reply when at the reception of the Knights it was demanded of them that they should renounce the crucified one.

It was not with denial of the Cross that the Cathars were

charged. They rejected nothing in the articles of faith. They did not disown Christ son of the Virgin, but the man whom Pilate crucified. And the vow of denial was made not only in France where the Inquisition obtained no matter what response by torture, but in England where torture was not pushed as far, or even used at all.

On all the evidence, the Templars made a distinction between the Christ and the crucified. Did documents found in Palestine teach them that in the first beginnings of Christianity, when the Church was as yet but a difference of opinion with the Synagogue, confusion was created, intentionally, between the 'Son of the Word' and the man who was crucified for having striven against the Romans and provoked disorder and rebellion by claiming his own kingdom as King of the Jews, descendant of David?

Or was it rather a question of putting a stop to that morbid complacency over a punishment to describe the horrors of which gave religious speakers a kind of pleasure? What was it that fascinated the makers of the Pietá?

However this may be, there is no crucified Christ in a cathedral of the XIIth and XIIIth centuries.

Chartres is a place of birth, not at all a place of death; and even the 'devils' with which it so much amused sculptors to startle kings and bishops make only a discreet appearance at the South door; more, it would seem, to divert the good people than to frighten them.

20 Three Roses

It is true that the cathedral is not entirely what it was: clerical and anti-clerical vandalism have passed that way. They first smashed windows and broke up the screen; others made an attack on the porticos. Someone tricked out the choir with a *'tour'* which is a museum-piece, nothing to do with the temple. The high altar was moved from the sacred place, first to the sanctuary, then to the crossing of the transepts. It was made to quit the mystical table, the table of the Last Supper, for the square, where the priest turns his back to the influx from Earth and Heaven. It is no longer an ascent to Golgotha but a toboggan-run. They have stuffed the church with loud-speakers. Discourse replaces the Word and the round table is blocked with chairs to help the slumbers of the right-thinking.

One need not be too astonished. The Age is drawing to a close, its religious forms with it. According to the National Geographical Institute's map of the sky, the vernal equinoctial point will cease to be in the constellation of Pisces, sign of the Christian era, towards the year 2010 – in forty-four years. There is therefore no need to be shocked if rituals are 'boiled to rags'.

All guides cite the cathedral at Chartres as a model of aesthetic achievement. But the master-craftsman was seeking something quite other than this. He was not creating Art but a cathedral. He was trying (and he succeeded) to construct an instrument of religious action, direct action, having in itself power over men; a power to transform and to transmute.

It is a means of passage from one world to another; a bridge between two worlds which, geometrically speaking, express themselves differently. It is a passage from the straight to the curved, as difficult to bring about as the marriage of fire and water. And it would seem that it is this successful transfer from the plane to the curve, this magic in the negation of weight by weight, this tension in stone that generated energy; this subtle projection of a celestial harmony that lives in matter, that is responsible, through man's grossest and subtlest senses at the same time, for this action.

Unless he is totally impervious, whoever has seen, or visited, Chartres is saturated with it, no longer quite the same man; and this in spite of the clutter of chairs, in spite of electrically stuttered prayers (and where now is the 'true voice'?), in spite of stupefying hymns in this monument to intelligence, in spite of all this the old 'crucible' has not lost all of its power.

At the beginning of this century a man came on foot from Paris by the old pilgrim's way. He was not among the foremost of believers, but, sprung from the sacred earth of Bélisama, a strange yeast fermented in him. He was called Péguy. He was of Orleans and found himself engaged in social conflicts that overwhelmed him. He came, simply, to put a sick child in the protection of Notre-Dame. He no more than another could remain the same after this pilgrimage. But he came 'open', in all the humility of his pride as a man. He was a poet and rhythm reached into the deepest regions of his being. He became the Singer of Notre-Dame-de-Chartres.

In fact the direct action of this monument is not yet extinct. But how much greater must it have been when the cathedral stood there in its original purity!

'I have never seen,' wrote a canon of last century, 'the interior of our cathedral in all its beauty but once: the day after the fire in 1836, when all that was movable had been removed . . .'

But we must follow man's progress through the cathedral as it was in the time of its simplicity, its primitive nakedness.

There are three ways in through the great West Door but only one route to follow; for the side doors open, not on the aisles, as in most other great churches, but all three on the nave.

To the right is the gate of birth over which Mary, Christian incarnation of the divine Mother, presides, seated like the Black Virgin with the Infant Deity on her knees. She is surrounded, within the curves of the arch, by the seven liberal Arts and by wise men who made them illustrious: all of them no doubt distinguished by the idea of them that was prevalent at the time. Among them are two signs of the zodiac, isolated, Pisces and Gemini. The Gemini are the two knights behind a single shield of carbuncle; two knights of the Temple, united, paired, as it were for duty according to the Rule, for which the Order held Notre-Dame in especial veneration. Pisces, the age when it reigned under this Sign.

On the left is the Gate of the Ages, presided over by an Ascension of Christ on a cloud upheld by two angels. In the surrounding arches we see the signs of the zodiac alternating with the works of man. The works of the twelve months are in good order; not so Pisces or Gemini.

In the centre is the Door of Mystical Faith — at least, so I would interpet it — between the works of nature and the work of the spirit. In the tympanum is that admirable Christ, blessing, between four evangelical winged symbols. He stands over the twelve apostles, ranged three by three, and the twenty-four old men of the Apocalypse. Among them one notices an Adept carrying a 'matrass' or long-necked vessel with rounded body used for distilling, mentioned by Fulcanelli in *Le Mystère des Cathédrales*.

There again we find three ways roofed by the ogive; the

ogive of the Door of Chartres, which fulfils its part so well
that the master-craftsman, although it was there before his
time, preserved it. Its part is to put a man on his feet,
upright, in the pride of his quality as a man, a quality
which would never exclude humility before the divine
world. Man's humility before man is baseness; want of
humility before the Universe is stupidity. To enter a
gothic church man does not stoop, he stands erect as God
meant him to.

He enters.

And he is suddenly in a different aspect of his own
world; in a world where the more a stone weighs the
lighter it is; where weight is its own negation; where what
was heavy takes wing; where no line bends a man but on
the contrary exalts him; where everything speaks to him of
earth in its hardest phase, stone, yet at the same time
reveals the Spirit of Earth to him, its harmony, its singing,
its divine essence. Here then he is, oblivious of his weight,
erect, lightened by the evocative, the mimetic power of
those stone shafts; here among telluric and cosmic forces
where he hears in himself the vibrating note, the 'La', of
his own close affinity with the entire world.

He is upright, that man who approaches the altar, in the
course of the telluric current, ineffable gift of the Earth
Mother, the Black Virgin, Saint Anne, Our Lady. And now
he stands before the round table, the Labyrinth.

Other labyrinths are extant, as at Amiens. The labyrinth
at Reims has fallen to ruins because urchins found it
amusing to run in and out of it. This irritated the canons.
These urchins — they could have chosen worse ground for
their games and the canons could rather have encouraged
them.

The name 'labyrinth' was given to these patterns drawn
on the flagstones, no doubt, because of a certain com-

plexity in the design. Sometimes they were called a
'daedalus', after the Minoan architect, father of Icarus, to
whom he gave wings. Legend is not groundless!

Much has been said about the symbolism of these
labyrinths. It is beyond doubt alchemical, but one cannot
fail to notice that the labyrinth at Chartres (no more than
those at Amiens and, formerly, at Reims) is not a labyrinth
properly speaking since it is impossible to get lost in it
because there is only one path and it leads to the centre.
All known labyrinths in a Notre-Dame shew this same
path, which is thus *fixed* and not left to the master-
craftsman or the master-paviour. This implies that it was
regarded as essential that the men who worked on a
'daedalus' should follow a given plan, one path and not
another. Let there be no doubt that this path must be
taken in rhythm, according to a ritual. But a ritual progress
is not a mere walk; it is a dance. A labyrinth is a
dance-pattern written on the ground; a reasoned version of
the qualities of the round or circle.

Reflect on it. We are now in a place that was chosen for
human utilisation of a telluric current that surfaces and
must have close analogies with currents that are magnetic.
Now, it is a well-known effect of an electric current that
all bodies in movement through its field acquire particular
properties. This is in fact the way electricity is made, by
causing a rotor to revolve in a magnetic field, natural or
artificial.

It is known too that the human body, immersed in such
a field — for example the spirals of a solenoid through
which an electric current is flowing — and thus plunged up
to the chest in a strong magnetic stream, is subjected to a
power that works profoundly in the body — fever brought
on for instance. Soft iron becomes magnetic. And if you
turn a man about in such a field in a given way, this will cause
given movements on his part.

THE LABYRINTH OF CHARTRES

A path written on the ground . . . and perhaps a gradual evolution in the man who takes it.

One might well — but does it matter? — recall to the simple-minded that to find one's way through the labyrinth was, for those who could not, a little like making the pilgrimage to Jerusalem (and much could be said about the 'road to Jerusalem'). The essential thing was that the labyrinth should be traversed.

Evidently it had to be accomplished unshod; not by way of penance but so that the feet should be in direct contact with the stone, which was an accumulator for the properties of the current. Just as the mud at Dax must be rubbed on the skin.

'Take thy shoes from off thy feet,' says Scripture, 'for the place whereon thou standest is holy ground.' And shoes must always be removed in a mosque. And gypsies always dance with bare feet.

It is likely that the ritual progress had to be made above all at times when the telluric current was in strong pulsation, which should coincide with the times of pilgrimage. In the spring certainly, as the 'Easter rounds', led by the Bishop, suggest.

The man who reaches the centre of the labyrinth, having made the ritual progress through it and having 'danced', is changed and for all I know in the sense that there has been an opening of the intuition to natural laws and harmonies; to laws and harmonies that he will perhaps not understand but which he will experience in himself, with which he will feel in tune and which will be for him the best test of truth as the diapason is the 'test' for a musician.

It is hardly likely that even when the *Wouivre* was in pulsation men were often visited by the Great Illumination. But to be in a receptive state is already more than most men can claim for themselves.

And now having accomplished the 'Road to Jerusalem' the pilgrim advanced to the square table.

The original pavement has as I said disappeared. 'Still,' says Bulteau, 'at several points, above all the crossing and at the foot of the nave, there are arrangements of

THE SQUARE TABLE AT AMIENS

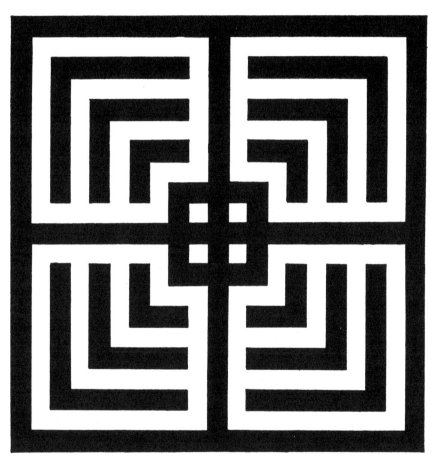

The sides of the table at Amiens are parallel or perpendicular to the axis of the cathedral. It is probable that the table at Chartres had one of its diagonals on this axis. One may suppose that the different parts of the table offered to those who found themselves there particularly revealing views of the ensemble of harmonies in stone which the monument expressed.

flagstones for which it is impossible to assign a reason.'
These are now to be found, those at the crossing at least,
under the new altar. It is probable that originally it was
not only a question of an arrangement of flagstones. One
can form an idea of the square table by reference to the
table at Amiens which is still at the entrance to the choir.

If one recalls the decimal relationships which link the
square table in the plan of Chartres with the table of the
great pyramid of Cheops, one finds it less extraordinary
that the table at Amiens should resemble the vertical
projection of a pyramid. It is here, in the middle of the
crossing of the transepts, that all the Numbers expressed in
the cathedral become perceptible; it is here that they can
be apprehended by the senses. Here all lines run together;
all proportions declare themselves. Here Numbers sing. It is
here too that they can be 'rationalised' — by those who
perceive them — under the fire of the three great roses.

The mystery of the 'roses' in gothic cathedrals remains
unbroken.

One knows that any idea of art for art's sake must be
abandoned. It is certain that they were put there for the
sake of their action, as part of the 'instrument'. This is
particularly noticeable at Chartres in respect of the great
western rose-window.

The master-craftsman found himself in face of a
problem extremely difficult to adjust: how to preserve, in
the western facade, the original doorway of 1155 which
doubtless exactly answered its purpose; how likewise to
preserve the triple window for the quality of its glass and
at the same time to include in the totality a *necessary*
western rose. To resolve this problem he was obliged to
distort the vaulting between the two towers and in a
manner imperceptible to the eye; to accentuate a slope of
the ground towards the doorway that one notices in the
cathedral and literally to obliterate one after the other the
three external stages of the facade, doorway, window and rose.

This could not be done without creating a certain

disharmony between the horizontal lines of the towers and the facade between them. The master-craftsman made the best compromise; but, when one notes, throughout the rest of the monument, the strictness with which line and proportion are linked in an implacable logic, one is forced to conclude that the 'rose' was put there under necessity and not by aesthetic compulsion. It is certain that it performed some useful function and the fact that the reason for it escapes us makes no difference.

For Fulcanelli these roses had their alchemical implications. 'The rose, then, represents, by itself,' he writes in *Les Demeures Philosophales**, 'the action of the fire and its duration. That is why mediaeval decorators sought to express in their rosaces the movements of matter quickened by elementary fire, as one may see over the North door of the cathedral at Chartres, in the roses at Toul . . .'

The three roses at Chartres present, as well, a peculiarity I believe exceptional: they are of stone hollowed to receive the glass and not, like those of other cathedrals, of stones put together to fit them.

However this may be, it is only at the crossing of the transepts, at the square table that is, that one can perceive the influx of light from the three windows simultaneously. And we must note that in the days when the screen was still there the light from the high windows in the choir reached only as far as that, for, symbolically, the mystical table is closed and is entered only by a 'strait gate'. It was here that the Knights, horsemen of the *Cabale* those not admitted to the mystical table, stood waiting. Here too the cathedral 'spoke' to the intellect, for this — and not in a symbolical sense alone — is the place of measures and comparisons and I do not doubt that the patterns on the flagstones were a key to it.

Three paths come to the crossing of the transepts and end there; symbolically they correspond with three states

* Pauvert, 1964.

of the human being who has already undergone evolution.

By way of the nave, which is the 'natural' route, a man did not come to the square table, that of 'comprehension', until he had passed the round table; after having known a new birth of some sort, having sloughed his human egocentricity in order to integrate himself as an active party in the harmony of terrestrial and cosmic forms and forces.

By way of the South-East transept, by the door known as the Door of the Knights, which is guarded by two knights with their feet *en equerre*, a door reserved symbolically for those instructed in the Cabale, who 'mounted' the Cabale, those that is who were instructed in the knowledge of law and natural harmonies. It is here that we must look for the origin of the legend that conferred on certain people the right of entry into churches 'on horseback'; a legend read literally by some thick-headed horsemen who thought they were knights.

This south-east entry is the door for initiates of the new covenant, the Christian era. The Christ who presides at the central door is a Christ who teaches. The closed book he holds has the exact proportions of the Golden Number, whereas the book Saint John holds at the same door has the proportions of the mystical table, 1/2.

The third path leads by way of the North-west transept, to which access is gained by the door called the door of the Initiates. It has a mysterious connexion with alchemy. On the pier of the central door is Saint Anne, mother of the Mother. Anne is indeed the supreme Mother, not unlike the Gaea of the Greeks. For the alchemists she is the womb from which all things issue and the whole entry is dedicated, with her, to esoteric Christianity, the left-hand door being consecrated to the Virgin whose 'dormition' in the tympanum makes one think, without constraint, of the verses which end Solomon's Song of Songs:

Oh, awaken not the Beauty until the time comes.

At the right-hand door, consecrated, it is said, 'to figures of the Old Testament who symbolise Jesus,' one notices that the tympanum is occupied by Job on his dunghill, which seems to me to represent symbolically, if it is not a rebus, putrefaction preparatory to rebirth in the distilling vessel. But only an Adept is qualified to interpret the whole of this entrance.

The stained-glass windows, the long lancets under the great rose, are no less eloquent. The middle window represents yet again Saint Anne, carrying the infant Virgin; a Saint Anne with black face who holds a stalk of flowering lily as well. She is surrounded by Melchisedek above Nebuchadnezzar, David above Saul, Solomon above Jeroboam and Aaron above Pharaoh. An allusion to alchemy is obvious in this.

It is likely that this door was reserved for philosophers who were making a study of the Great Work.

The mystical table, enclosed in the choir, was shut off. As now, there are two ways of access, reserved for officiants, to the left of the choir, near the sanctuary.

Before this door likewise the pavement has been altered. It too was marked with a square table, such as the one at Amiens, which is still in place: thus, the officiants themselves went in by a representation of the square table. The mystical table was not accessible to the ignorant.

The other entrance, a narrow door contrived in the central arcade of the screen, was at the head of the square table at the crossing of the transepts. To pass through it was to renounce the material world. It was to achieve the third birth that follows the second death. Here, all ceremonial was secret. It was only later that the public was admitted to the celebration of the rite.

Throughout his journey a man who entered the

cathedral was bathed in telluric emanations, sonorous, visible, luminous, in which the magical effects of the ritual — for a rite is magical, whatever name one cares to give it — took on an astonishing amplitude and power, so that the man felt himself profoundly affected. And if the rite, now debased, has lost much of its power; if the disappearance of a number of protective stained-glass windows renders the sun's light destructive; if loud-speakers sound strangely false, still more so the hymns that are sung in this place that was built for faultless harmony; its architectural harmony remains intact, or little short of it and no man can boast, not even in a practical sense, that he leaves the cathedral at Chartres the same as he was when he went in.

21 The Third Measure

There are three tables in Chartres Cathedral.

There are also three plans.

The first is the plan of enclosure, the superficial limits, the extent of the place. It has two easily analysed dimensions. The unit of measurement or 'module' is one of 0.82 metres.

The second is so to speak the plan of the 'void', and it takes in the architecture of the elevation, which is why the unit of measurement used for building is that of the second plan. It concerns the main vessel only. The aisles, like the deambulatory, are but means of passage, not stages on the initiatory path. It is a harmonic design involving geographical lines, musical sounds and the colours of light. It is linked with the position of Chartres on the terrestrial globe and an organisation of volumes entailed. It has three dimensions and the 'measure' is one of 0.738 metres.

I have not gained any knowledge of the third plan, but only the conviction that it exists. Perhaps it has no measure in terms of length, for if it is interposed with the other two it lies beyond the apparent inertia of matter. It can only have to do with living matter, in movement. Logically, it should be a plan in four dimensions in which time plays a part.

It is a plan in movement, for everything in the cathedral moves, the counter-movements of stones taut as springs, neutralising instantly each other's movement. I have pointed out, as I was bound to do, the dynamic function of the crossed ogive. Its static appearance cannot hide that it constitutes a vault in vibration which by that very fact is in time, in a temporal space.

The cathedral vibrates to the slightest sound and, though this may be imperceptible to our senses, to the slightest pulsation of the telluric current of which it is the crowning achievement.

I have pointed out too how much further this dimensional relationship of the church with the flow of time extends: the length of the 'empty' vessel is a ten-thousandth part of its shift in one hour by rotation of Earth round its axis.

And all this proceeds from a plan that has likewise its own unit of measurement. But it is not easily decyphered, although the master-craftsman must certainly have left obvious clues, as he did for the other units. Perhaps they lie under one's very nose. They are without doubt the clues that enable one to open the doors to this kingdom of the essential harmony of Earth and Cosmos in movement; a harmony whose law is perhaps the solution of the universal equation that modern science seeks by weighing epiphenomena, an effort that limits it to being nothing other than the science of epiphenomena.

The cathedral itself was conceived with the aim of setting mankind in movement. In the calculated meanderings of the labyrinth that must be explored ritually; in the alignments of the square table, over which there probably was enacted the ritual of the 'lustral water', quickened by four breaths and over which some intellectual game in which Numbers are pushed from box to box ought still to be played — it might reveal the symbolism of the game of chess; in the rectangular table, secret place of the Christian ritual at the base of gesture and rhythm.

It goes without saying that this dissection into three

plans is but a method of analysis and that the three aspects of the building spring from a single and unique idea, as the cathedral springs from a centre and a plant from its seed, growing as it takes shape according to an over-riding law of harmony. And this way is the opposite of that which a man will be asked to take.

For a man, the cathedral is first of all an arrangement of matter as material as matter can be, stone, apparently immobile, unchangeable. Once inside the cathedral nothing of this remains but the enclosure of an emptiness and in the emptiness it changes aspect not according to surfaces but lines. And its linear development is resolved when it comes to a point, a point where all matter, all space, all surfaces, all movement, disappear.

Is it to be understood that it is only when a man, in the course of his wanderings, has abandoned all ties with matter that the key to the complexity of the Universe in its totality is shewn to him? When in traditional language he sees God face to face? The entire Universe in an atom as the atom is comprised in the Universe? To bring a man to the point, if not of understanding at least of communion with the World — that is the meaning and aim of the cathedral. It will be understood why I speak of a 'utilitarian monument'.

Christianity's greatest, most magnificent conquest has been to put at the disposal of all men an initiatory monument formerly reserved to a privileged few who alone had right of access to the inside of a temple.

There is plenty of magic in the cathedral of Chartres. Perhaps it is not to the cathedral itself but to its situation that we should ascribe the therapeutic properties that have been known throughout the West since the Middle Ages. We possess no document that justifies us in asserting that the medicinal qualities of the place, or of the water from the Celtic well, were known before Christianity, or even before the building of the present cathedral; but it is a fact that from the XIIth to the XVIth century the sick resorted there in the mass, to such a point that a kind of lazar-house was installed in the crypt, where patients were looked after in the bosom of Earth herself, close to the dolmenic chamber, with water from the well. The really ill, the paralytics above all, were healed there. The water was also efficacious for wounds.

This kind of magical action was felt not only inside the church. According to Froissart, in 1360 the King of England laid seige to the city of Chartres, having set up his camp near Bretigny, seven kilometres away. One morning when the sky was especially blue, the weather clement, he gave orders for the assault; but just then a storm, which no-one could have predicted, gathered right over the camp and precipitated itself. 'It hailed such great stones,' Froissart writes, 'that they killed men and horses and all were the more amazed.' Edward III, alarmed, raised his arms to the steeples of the cathedral and called on Notre-Dame to bring the cataclysm to an end, in return for which he would offer the King of France immediate peace. The storm passed and the sky grew serene again.

A miracle certainly. A miracle also the fact that ever since the cathedral was built some mode of occult protection seems to have been extended to the town, which escaped almost all the damage that arises from warfare. Even the destruction wrought by the wars of religion and the Revolution was mild enough: some themes in stone were smashed at the Royal Entrance — bishop and chapter wrought far worse — the revolutionaries contented themselves with pillaging the Treasure and taking lead from the roof to make republican cannon-balls. The fire of 1836 that ravaged the *forest*, that is to say the roof-timbers — did not get as far as to attack the vault, which is truly miraculous, nor to affect the windows.

Finally, it must be pointed out that during the

Revolution Chartres was in some sort a place of asylum where there lived in comparative security a number of aristocrats who in other places would have been condemned to public execution.

Many other things remain mysterious about this cathedral, whose simplicity and interior nakedness are so surprising.

Canon Bulteau, who last century published a monograph in two large volumes, points out that at the entrance to the labyrinth, fixed into a flagstone, there is a ring held by a piton and above this, painted on the vault, a red Maltese cross. If the ring has vanished the piton remains; but I can see no trace of the red cross painted on the wall above. The canon did not know the meaning and use of these signs. Neither do I.

There are on the southern wall of the South tower two highly damaged carvings: an ass holding an instrument of music and another animal, standing on its hind legs, whose head and front parts have disappeared. According to oral tradition, this is 'the Ass that plays the hurdy-gurdy' and the 'Sow that spins'. The sow is visibly a boar and the hurdy-gurdy a kind of cithern.

'What a strange thing,' Canon Bulteau writes, 'there is to be seen on a document from ancient Egypt, an ass that plucks (the French word is 'pince' and the author himself queries it) a lyre with nine strings.' Egypt again.

The ass is perhaps an onager, an animal which in antiquity had some symbolical meaning I have been unable to find. There are at least two 'asses' that are stars in the constellation of Cancer and for the Egyptians the ass symbolised Typhon, a god of evil.

Were we concerned with no more than a small carved stone we might have allowed ourselves to assume some malicious trick on the part of some sculptor who meant to mock those who are always wishful to do for music what they are as little fitted to do as the donkey, the harmony of whose voice is well known. But this piece of sculpture is of too much consequence for there to be any question of a joke. And then, there is the sow or boar, as to which we are better informed. The word *truie* is a variation of an ancient Celtic word (truth) that means *wild boar*. Truth, by phonetic assimilation, was one of the images of the Druid, not the only one: another was the oak, *dru*; yet another was connected with the trout. The 'boar that spins' is the Druid who draws a guiding thread from the distaff, like Ariadne's. Was there a tradition among the building confraternities of a druidic know-how carefully preserved in the tricks of their trade and its jargon? Certain survivals of Gaulish art, above all in romanesque architecture, make one think so.*

Finally, there is the mystery of the inviolable and inviolate Mound. Is the 'taboo' really connected with the quality of the earth and the telluric current? Who can say?

One has often enough noticed, in sacred places, the existence of three caverns or three crypts superimposed which might have corresponded, originally, with three stages of initiation. It would not be in the least bit astonishing if three caverns or traditional crypts existed beneath Chartres.

The subsoil at Chartres is honeycombed in every direction with very ancient underground caverns, most of which have been turned into septic tanks. Thus, during recent digging of foundations beneath a modern house-property facing the House of the Salmon there were found, according to one uncontradicted public rumour, *twelve* tiers of caves. Even allowing for customary exaggeration, it is certain that there were important cavities on this site, which is on the Mound, near the cathedral. It would be in no way astonishing if things were the same beneath the cathedral itself.

Was the 'taboo' designed to prevent access to a

* Marcel Moreau: La Tradition Celtique dans l'Art Roman. Atlantis.

hiding-place where some especially precious object lay buried? One thinks at once of the Ark of the Covenant which once lay among the foundations of Solomon's Temple.

It is worth while asking this question, for it seems clear that there must once have been a barrier of some sort near the cathedral, which is to say the least of it unusual.

The apse of the chapel of Saint-Piat, constructed at the end of the XIVth century, is saddled with two towers that share nothing in style with the chapel itself or any style that could be called religious. They could have been part of a small castle and this, it would seem, was the case. Besides, one of them, the northern one, stands exactly in the axis of the cathedral and might have served as guiding mark for the plan drawn on the ground. If one considers the plan from this tower, one 'sees' the apse at an angle of 90°, which is certainly not a matter of chance; and its distance from the doors of the cathedral (measured on the plan) is about 148 metres. I am inclined to correct this figure to 147.60 metres. The width of the transepts from the exterior columns of the North portico to those of the South is about 73.80 metres; thus, the geometrical mean of the two lengths, that make a rectangle in the proportion of 1/2, comprising the total area of the cathedral including the two towers just mentioned, is $\sqrt{147.6 \times 73.8}$ = about 104.40 metres or the height of the southern tower on the West side.

No doubt it could be deduced from this that the two towers on the East side, which as I hold were part of some defensive organisation, date from the same epoch. To add some form of direct and material defence to the 'taboo' may have been judged necessary.

It would be of extreme interest if we could find at least the sub-basements, the foundations, of the ensemble to which these two towers belonged. If it were found that it was squared to four *tours d'angle* this would amount to a

Templar signature. And one might remember that Wolfram d'Eisenbach created the Grand Master of the Temple Keeper of the Grail.

Here, as far as my knowledge will take it, ends this analysis of the Temple of the West.

Greater men than I will find greater things in it; if they do not lose themselves in the square table where cerebral speculations become idle, they well might, God helping them, discover the mode of transition from spatial into temporal rhythms. For the man who writes space writes time.

Whoever would reach the point where spatial rhythms offer a key to the temporal should seek the third, the secret measure, the 'ancient measure', which was the measure of the Pyramids and of Solomon's Temple.

It may seem amazing that there should be such correspondences between Cheops and Chartres; between two monuments so disparate, two forms of civilisation so far removed in space and time. It only *seems* astonishing.

Traditional science is a science in all the meanings this word may contain; more complete, certainly, than up-to-date science that with microscope and telescope never sees the Universe except from the outside, not possessing the *intus lectio*, the gift of reading from within (is not this the etymology of the intelligence?). And it is because of science, bestower of power, that such knowledge has been kept secret, hidden, occult. Occult, being dangerous, like all science to the man who uses it without conscience, it has never practically speaking emerged from 'colleges' and essentially religious brotherhoods, whatever the form of religion.

Scientific books in such colleges and brotherhoods are rebuses, enigmas, books of puns even, that one cannot hope to understand without having taken classes in every domain open to human faculties, the spiritual included; rebuses or enigmas that are legendary (as in mythology), sacred writings, carved stones, monuments.

But beneath the variety of rebus and enigma lies *one* science. Legends, sacred writings, carved stones and monuments have a common basis which is repeated from initiatory monument to initiatory monument, whether in certain dolmens, pyramids, temples or cathedrals. (Has it been noticed that the empty spaces contrived in the pyramid of Cheops over the King's Chamber,. which are supposed to be lumber rooms, were in fact dolmenic chambers, five dolmens one over the other?).

To come across identical proportions in such various monuments is less astonishing than it seems since the great law of harmony which they express is one law, even if the style is different. It is no more astonishing than that these monuments should be found in places where telluric currents can help men to achieve intelligence, the *intus ligere*, the reading from within of Great Nature, visible symbol of the Great Law. Just as much as nature, science is a unity that reaches from pyramid to cathedral; and this is why there are so many coincidences between the proportions of Chartres and those of Cheops.

Among others, we know that the King's Chamber in the great pyramid has the following dimensional proportions: width, 1; length, 2; height, 1.117. If you multiply these figures by 16.4, you get: width, 16.4; length, 32.8; height, 18.32. Now, 18.32 x 2 = 36.64 and 36.64 metres is the height of the vault above the choir at Chartres, whose rectangular table has a width of 16.4 metres and a length of 32.8. Which is to say that the choir at Chartres is directly linked in its proportions with the King's Chamber.

If dimensions and proportions repeat themselves, it is nevertheless obvious that the two monuments are not copies one of the other. There must then have been a *different* application of the same science. This implies possession of the same key; but it implies as well — and this is really distressing — a knowledge of the laws of an evolution which condition the means of action from which a style flows. But perhaps this too is contained in the key.

As to this key or clue, one sees traces of it easily enough in history, even when what one is after looks like legend. To go no further back, it persists from the Pyramids to Moses, who wrote it on the Tables of the Law; it passes from David to Solomon, his son, who was 'instructed in all the wisdom of the Egyptians (Kings)' and used it for the building of his Temple. The *Document de Damas* tells that the Saviour had knowledge of it. The Persian adepts seem not to have overlooked it after Jerusalem fell to Islam. The nine first Knights Templar handed it to the Cistercians, who drew from it the three initiatory *Notre Dame*.

Then it was hidden once again and will so remain until the right time shall come, for the growth of civilisations follows a temporal rhythm, a pulsation of the great Seasons of the Eras. And we may note that there was a period of one Era between the Pyramids and Solomon's Temple, another between the Temple and Chartres.

Chartres was never finished.

This is not only a question of details regarding some pinnacles on the North portico. It has been suggested likewise that each of the blocking towers, two at the beginning of the apse, two at the ends of each transept, ought to be surmounted with an antenna and that a central spire should be added at the crossing. One such existed at one time, not in stone but in wood; it was burnt down in 1836. We do not know whether it was there from the beginning.

As to the other towers, this would seem improbable, because the north tower on the western front, although the first to be built, did not have one, and because according to the architects, Jean de Beauce, who built the northern spire, would have had to bring off a real *tour de force*, no tower capable of such a weight having yet been conceived. I myself believe there could have been only one spire at Chartres. The only sign of incompletion lies in the

abandonment of the stone-yard before the North portico
was finished, a thing that still has to be pointed out if it is
to be noticed. And it is only a question of external
decoration.

The 'instrument' itself was completed. It functioned.
Flourishes round its feet hardly affect the sonority of a
piano.

But in 1260 or thereabouts, when the workmen
abandoned the North portico, they were already no longer
just workmen. They were remarkable in other respects.
Free. Having obtained their immunities. Free and responsible to themselves. In other stoneyards attached to the
Church, men only worked sporadically.

It seems to be the case that towards this time, or
perhaps earlier, there was a general loss of spirit. Spirit had
finished with the Gothic. Men were about to build the
'ogival', with all the flourishes of virtuosity. They were
about to make Art for Art's sake.

All went as if, the initiatory monument once completed,
men were given back their entire and arbitrary freedom,
like school-children when lessons are over. Let them live
their lives at their own risk!

This withdrawal of spirit did not affect only the
builders. A Cistercian monk, a chief of the Order, led a
crusade against the Albigenses. The terrible phrase, 'Kill
them all! God will recognise his own!' is attributed to him.
If this is not true, the fact that the phrase can be ascribed
to him shews clearly enough the spirit in which he
conceived his part. The Dominicans, preaching brothers,
invented the Inquisition and grew fat on it. The trial of the
Templars shews into what poverty of spirit men had fallen.
Jewish history shews that it was just the same when, the
Temple being completed, Solomon disappeared.

The book once opened, men are free.

The Beauty sleeps. But her castle remains hidden among

its thorns.

The 'Hand' that directs the evolution of worlds always leaves one monument as a lighthouse. If men will be blind, that is their choice; if they will see, the means of sight is always left to them with full liberty of action. They are free. They are responsible. Individually.

And when not one just man is left the book closes and the Temple collapses.

AFTERWORD

Born in 1905, Louis Charpentier, journalist, traveller, author and publisher, has travelled on foot through Egypt and Libya and has carried out researches in antiquity for the Public Works Department of the International Administration of Tangiers. It was while discussing the action of the megaliths on the behaviour of animals and plants that he came to the study of 'traditional sciences' or systems of knowledge. He is particularly interested in the history of the Knights Templar, which gave rise to the construction of Chartres Cathedral.

Some fifty years before this book was published, the late Frederick Bligh Bond, F.R.I.B.A., was unveiling the same theme in his excavation at Glastonbury Abbey, but the Abbey Trustees refused to accept his findings, and he went to America. Elizabeth Leader and Janette Jackson, M.B.E., who had both carried on studies concerning Glastonbury as their private research, invited Keith Critchlow, A.R.C.A., to make an independent assessment of the work. In 1967 Critchlow championed Bligh Bond and his geometrical principle, thus indicating a link between Chaldea, Egypt, Persia and Judah with Stonehenge, the Somerset Zodiac and the Gothic cathedrals — especially the beautiful example of the Glastonbury Lady Chapel.

In 1969 John Michell's *View Over Atlantis* presented these ideas to an even wider public. Finally, a small research group was formed under the leadership of Professor Mary Williams, M.A., D.U.P., *Officier, Legion d'Honneur*, and Commander G. Mathys, R.N., to provide a platform for other forms of investigation.

Our forebears have left these records in stone, which cannot be repeated today, despite present technical brilliance, but of the people and their cities we know little. Their greatest achievements were accomplished without disturbing ecological balance. In contrast, man is now generally recognized to be set on a course which, if not halted, could destroy all forms of life on this earth. The Research Into Lost Knowledge Organisation is dedicated to making such matters better considered, while trying to get Bligh Bond, and other early pioneers, the recognition which is their due.